rlboro
oro

FORMULA ONE RACING

with Marlboro McLaren Mercedes

Marlboro
MIKA
Marlboro
EAGLE

FORMULA ONE RACING

with Marlboro McLaren Mercedes

Norman Howell

photography by

Crispin Thruston

Marlboro
Benz
TENCEL
McLAREN INTERNATIONAL
FOCA

SÃO PAULO SÃO PAULO
9 9
BRAKES ON
BOSS
McLAREN INTERNATIONAL
speedline

Contents

TENCEL
Mobil
1
7
COURTAULDS
EAGLE

Family Tree

Formula One teams vary greatly in size. From Forti Corse, run on a shoe-string, to McLaren and Ferrari, where huge resources are available. Most teams exist somewhere in between these extremes. The end goal for each is to have three cars at every Grand Prix, with enough spares and a competent enough driver to take his car to the end without costly accidents. For the wealthier end of the grid, the goal is to have the tiniest of advantages in order to to win, or at the very least, score points.

The larger outfits will be made up of a test team as well as a race team. The former will be quite independent from the latter, often testing immediately before and immediately after a Grand Prix. The only crossover will be represented by the drivers – though the top four teams have their own test drivers too – and some of the race engineers. This, as can be imagined, is very expensive. Even fairly large middle ranking teams cannot afford this kind of outlay. They do test of course, but necessarily less so, as the mechanics can only put in so many working days during the course of a season.

Thus while McLaren has one half of the test team, with their test driver, doing straight line aerodynamic and speed testing

Michael Negline and one of the three 'babies' which are his responsibility throughout the season.

A thoughtful Steve Hallam, Mika Hakkinen's race engineer.

at a circuit in France, the rest of the test team is in Portugal evaluating other data on track with the two race drivers. Meanwhile, the race team engineers and mechanics are back at the factory in England working and preparing for the next Grand Prix, as well as evaluating the data that is being sent over from the two test sessions. Not many teams can reach these levels of concentration. One can imagine how much easier a problem is to identify and then solve if this kind of manpower and logistical resources can be deployed. Spare a thought for the smaller teams. Some go testing with the race team personnel. Others use the Friday pre-qualifying session as their own test session: it's the only time they can afford to do so.

Most teams are structured along broadly similar lines, especially the British ones. The national divisions were greater once, but now, what with Ferrari and Ligier sporting a large number of British staff, this is no longer the case. The management structure can be different though and this sometimes does make a crucial difference, especially in the decision-making process.

The line of command in the pits is very clear and well defined. Discipline is very important as things have a tendency to happen very quickly and it is importantant to avoid the 'headless chicken' syndrome.

Each race car is assigned three mechanics. It is their baby for the whole season. They build it up before each race, and they strip it down in the factory after each Grand Prix. They know everything about it. Then comes a 'number one' mechanic. He is in charge of the car. He will report directly to the chief mechanic, who in turn is responsible for the mechanics on all the cars. He will relay to the number one mechanic of each car the instructions of the race engineers during qualifying sessions, when things have to be altered mechanically on the car. The chief mechanic at McLaren is Michael Negline and he will liaise with Steve Hallam and David Brown, the race engineers, on what is to be done. At the end of the session, and after debriefing, Negline will be handed a job list by the race engineers and will then decide how to best deploy his staff for the

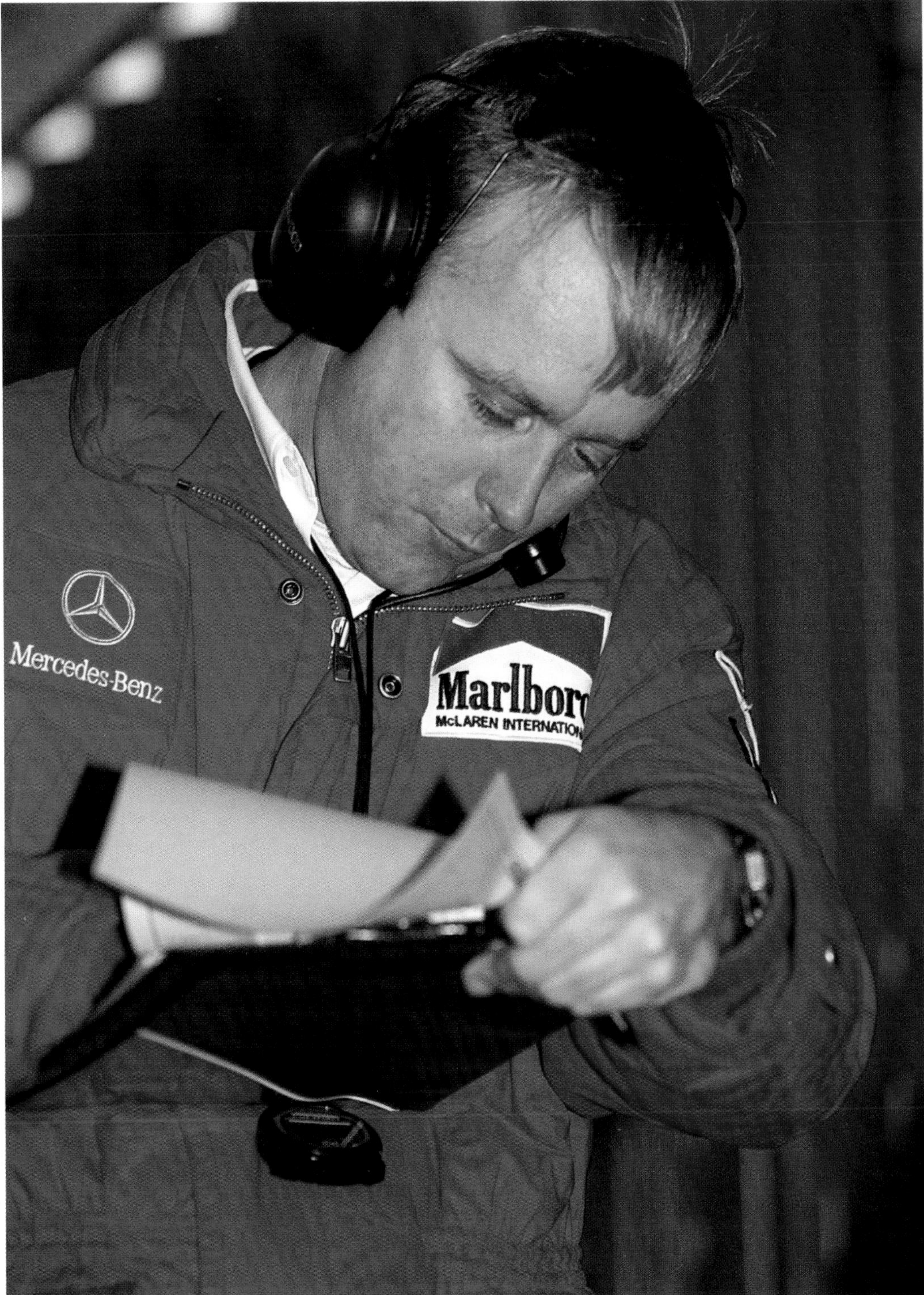

David Brown, David Coulthard's race engineer, takes note of Coulthard's comments.

long working hours ahead. In this he will be helped by the team manager, David Ryan, who is in charge of the whole race team at each Grand Prix. This includes all the people assigned to the cars. In addition there are the truckdrivers, workshop personnel and anyone else who is involved with the cars. He attends debriefing sessions and, as a senior member of the team, plays an active part in the race team effort.

From this point 'upwards', however, the hierarchy gets a little more hazy. Nominally

A rare smile from David Ryan, the McLaren team manager who carries many of the team's problems on his shoulders throughout the season.

Ryan is in charge for the duration of the weekend. Together with the senior engineers he will decide how many sets of tyres to use, when it is best to send a driver out for his qualifying lap and generally set the pattern for the team's tactics for the weekend. This pattern is repeated with most team managers up and down the pit lane. But McLaren has a very hands-on team principal, Ron Dennis, who loves the business of racing and to get involved in the decision-making process. He is very good at it – at times he has the touch of genius. But of course he also makes mistakes. He is reluctant to empower those around him, as he feels he can do things better. The result of this is that the race team is run by Ryan until Sunday, when Dennis takes over. This can be for the good, or for the worse. It does, though, create a certain degree of confusion and frustration.

To complicate matters more, the factory at Woking is run by the operations director, Martin Whitmarsh, who has wide-ranging powers exceeding those normally associated with a factory manager. This is partly due to his strong personality and partly due to Dennis, who has encouraged him to take some of the load off his own shoulders. One driver who was recently employed by McLaren commented he was surprised to be in a team that is run by Whitmarsh during the week, by Ryan at the circuit until Sunday, which is when Dennis takes over. He thought it didn't work too badly, but that the potential for confusion was greater than in other teams, where the lines of communication and command were more distinct.

Working alongside the team manager there is the team co-ordinator, Joe Ramirez, who is in charge of all the logistics of the team. In charge of the race engineers is Neil Oatley, the chief designer, who also has reporting to him aerodynamicists and systems engineers. There is also a marketing company, Tag McLaren Marketing Services, which is run by Ekrem Sami. It is somewhat bigger than any marketing unit in Formula

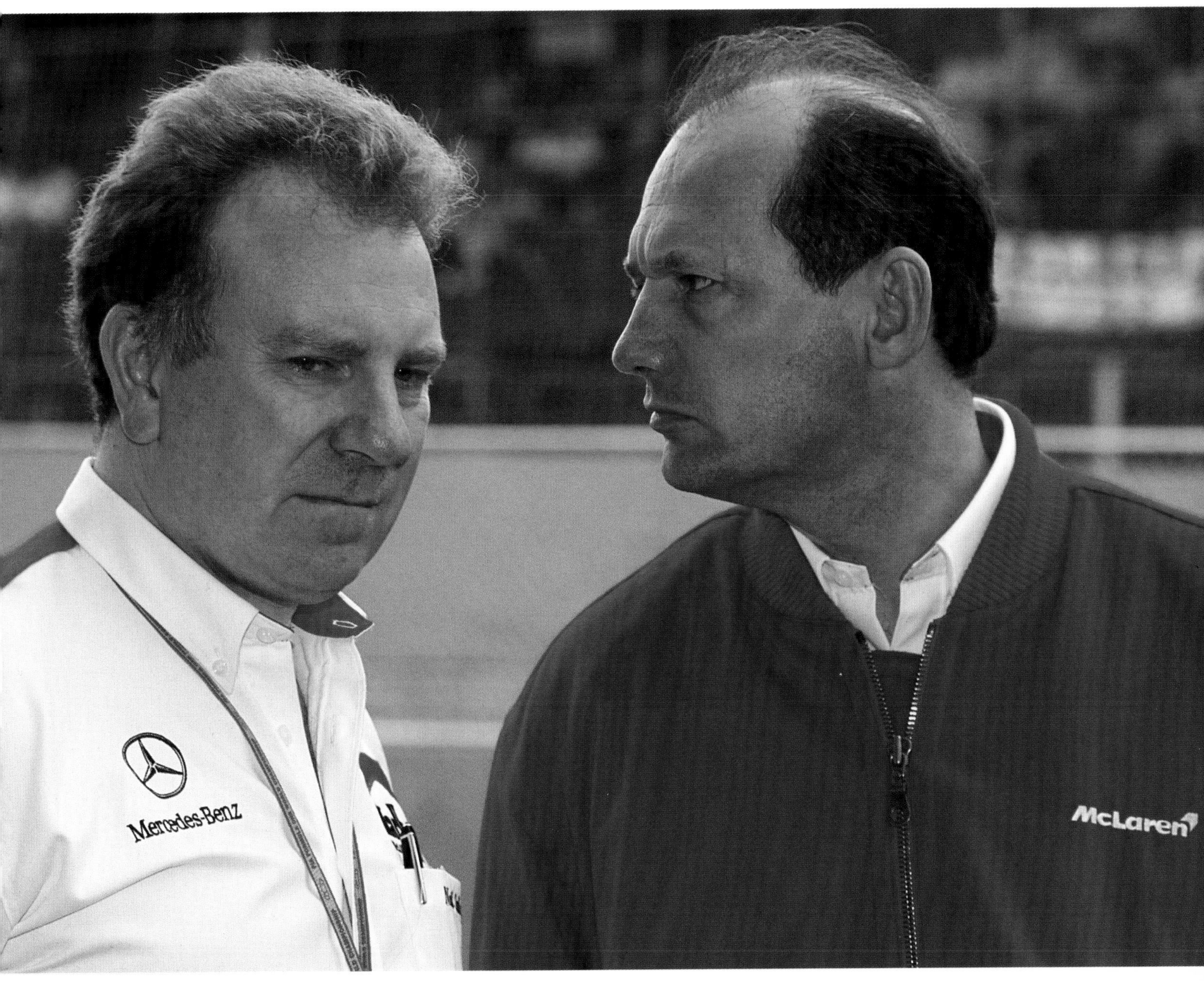

Neil Oatley (left), McLaren's chief designer, and Ron Dennis, team principal, put their heads together to solve one of the many engineering puzzles which arise during a Grand Prix.

One. This is because it covers a wide area, from VIP hospitality to motor home staff, to the media, business acquisition and design. But also because the underlying philosophy in a team like McLaren is that the bigger it is, the better it must be. It has worked for many years, but, by Dennis' own admission, there is a certain amount of dead wood which should not be in the team. Dennis also admits, however, to being sentimental and finding it hard to get rid of people. As people are paid extremely well at McLaren, this has led to a situation where people will not leave. Therefore the upper reaches of the company have not had any new blood for quite some time, and this is probably detrimental to the cause of McLaren's long-term revival.

At McLaren there is also a Home Team, made up of all the people who are essential to the race effort but who are factory based. Many are former race team mechanics who

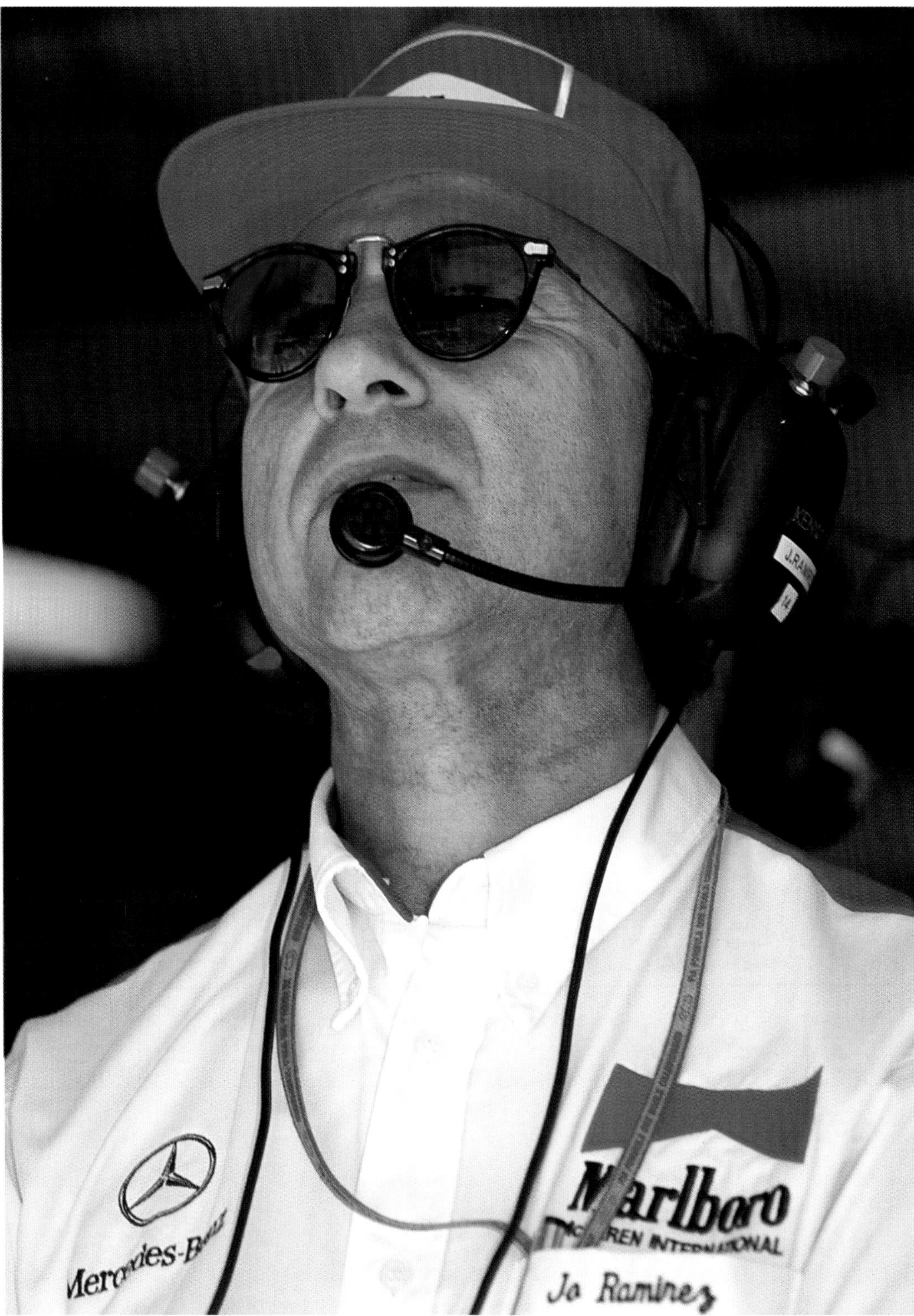

Joe 'Cool' Ramirez, team co-ordinator, is seen by many in the paddock as the friendly face of McLaren.

have decided to spend more time with their families and have therefore opted for a more sedentary job. One of them is Neil Trundle, who runs the gearbox shop. Actually he is a lot more than a former mechanic, as he was one of Dennis' original partners. Trundle's gearboxes are incredibly reliable, each component is tracked, each gear has its 'life expentancy' carefully monitored. Practically everything is done in-house, down to the gears, which are precision-cut with the help of a special Swiss machine and the use of water.

The desire to handle as much work as possible in-house stems from the need to control the quality of the components which will find their way into the race car. Thus the need to hire more and more people and the necessity of finding larger premises. The whole of the McLaren group of companies – comprising an electronic division and the F1 road car, as well as the marketing and race team – employs about 550 people. The employees of McLaren International, strictly speaking the Formula One team, are 270.

All of this cannot guarantee success, of course. In fact the sheer numbers at Dennis's disposal are an encouragement to throw 'money and bodies' at a problem, instead of using a more surgical approach. But this is the nature of the team and for a long while it was a system that worked admirably. Undoubtedly though, the McLaren tree could do with a little pruning and maybe then a few young shoots would grow to help the team towards new thinking and new victories.

The three McLaren drivers in relaxed and jovial mood. On the left Mika Hakkinen, on the right David Coulthard, and in the middle Jan Magnussen, the team's official test driver.

A Formula One car is made of more than 3,000 components. Each one has to be designed, built and tested before it can be fitted to the car.

The new car takes shape in the design office on a powerful computer.

For most of the teams competing in the 1996 Formula One Grand Prix championship, the real start of the season was not in Australia; it wasn't even during the first testing sessions in February. The 1996 season started in August 1995, when the designers sat themselves in front of a blank computer screen and began to flesh out the new car.

Every year the Fédération Internationale de l'Automobile (FIA), the sport's governing body, tweaks the Formula One rules, usually in the interest of safety. This means the designers have to begin again using these new rules as the bedrock from which to build a new car. A Formula One car is made of more than 3,000 components. Each one has to be designed, built and tested before it can be fitted to the car.

This is an awesome task, which requires great organization and attention to detail. McLaren has a chief designer who heads a group of project leaders, each one in charge of crucial areas of the car such as aerodynamics, chassis, transmission and so on.

The car begins to take shape on the computer screens in early autumn. By now a scale model will have been built for wind tunnel testing. This model will be built reproducing the aerodynamic features of the new car. The detail is such that even the insides of the car, such as the engine and the exhaust system, are an exact replica of the full-size car. The testing in the wind tunnel is extensive and is crucial to the shape the car will ultimately take on the track. McLaren have invested much time and money in adapting the tunnel so that it can replicate a variety of conditions. This, allied with a testing rig which mirrors the behaviour of a racing car on any given race track in Formula One, provides the McLaren engineers with a massive amount of data. Their task is then to isolate and process this raw information into a meaningful and helpful structure on which to base the car's design.

The reliance on advanced technology for this stage of the car build is somewhat balanced by the appearance in one of the factory workshops of a full-size, wood-and-paper model: the 'touch and see factor' is still as important to the engineers, proof that this is still very much a creative process.

The first full-scale chassis is usually built by the end of January. This is the heart of the car. The driver sits in it and it is the basis for all of the safety systems on the final model. Before anything else can be fitted on to the chassis, it has to pass stringent crash tests prescribed by the FIA. Thus the chassis, and the nose cone, are subjected to violent deceleration as well as side-impact tests which must be passed if the car is to take part in the Formula One Championship. For some years

New Car

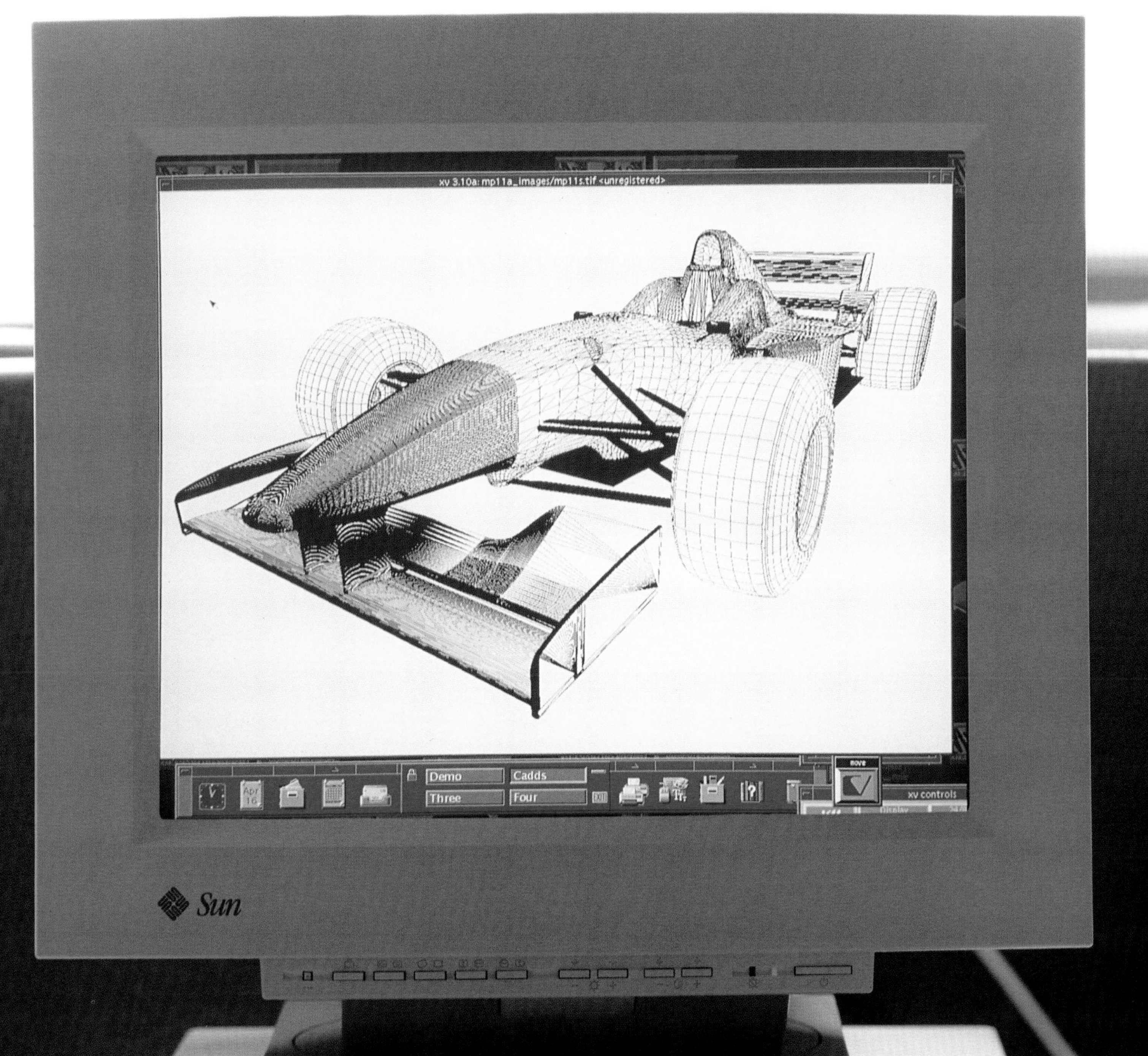
xv 3.10a: mp11a_images/mp11s.tif <unregistered>
Demo
Cadds
Three
Four
xv controls
Sun

(opposite top) Composite fibres are hand crafted by highly expert staff at McLaren's Woking factory.

now McLaren has been at the forefront in matters of safety. It was McLaren who first introduced the use of composite fibres, previously only employed in the aircraft industry. More recently McLaren have spearheaded research into special foam for the head restraints now mandatory on Formula One cars, as well as providing a chassis for research on the use of airbags for Grand Prix cars.

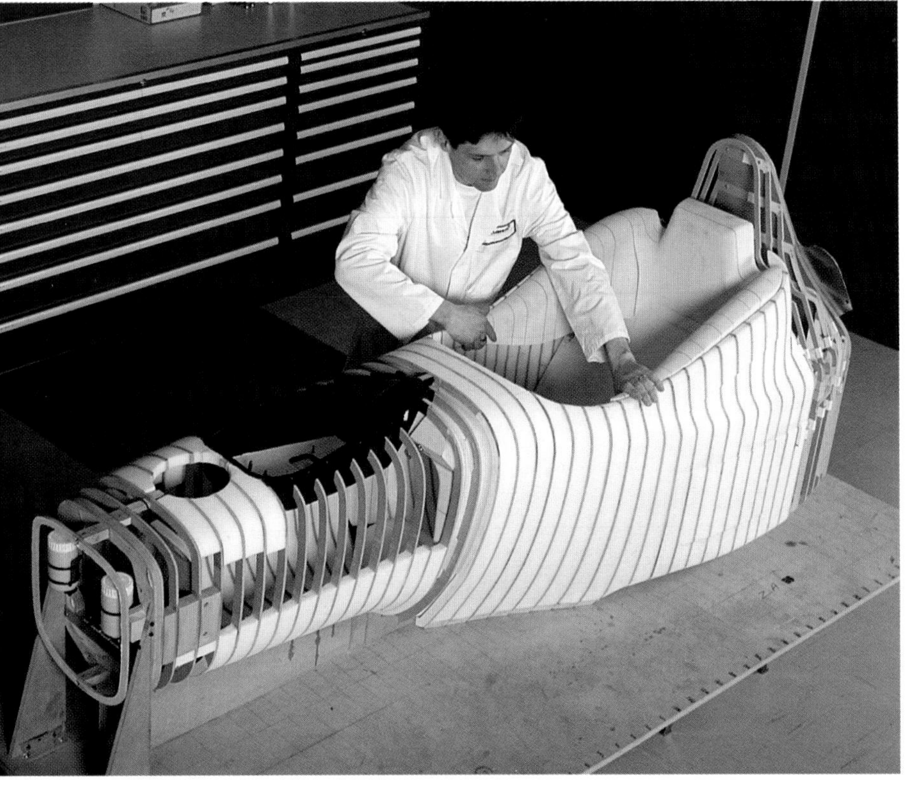

Old-fashioned wood and paper are still used so that engineers can get a 'see and feel' perspective of the car.

Once the chassis has been crash-tested, it goes back to McLaren where a group of mechanics are given the task of assembling the first of the five cars needed to start the season: three on track and two held in reserve. This is very much a start-stop time for the factory. Frenzied, all-night activity is followed by enforced moments of rest as crucial components are missing or are being prepared in one of the giant ovens, called autoclaves. Only when the chassis is fitted with the suspensions, the pushrods and eventually the wheels, does it really start to look like a racing car.

(opposite) Individual composite fibre components are then cured (baked) in the factory's autoclave (oven).

Meanwhile, crucial elements like the gearbox and the gear ratios are being built in-house. This is accomplished by a mixture of Computer Aided Design and Computer Aided Machining (CAD-CAM) as well as more traditional machining skills combined with the experience McLaren has acquired over 25 years of racing. All of these components are fitted to the chassis, as are the more visible elements like the engine cover and the aerodynamic wings.

Eventually the body parts are painted in the famous red-and-white colours. Each car will have two kilos of acrylic polyethene paint sprayed on it. The distinctive red contains special ultraviolet protective lacquer so that it will not fade under the sun.

When the car is finally assembled, fully painted, with the wheels and tyres on, the factory comes to a standstill. It shouldn't, as everyone has plenty of work to get on with now that the season is looming, but the excitement of seeing the new car finally 'born' is too much for most people. In dribs and drabs they file into the workshop, looking in wonder at the beautiful, sleek racing machine. This is the result of all the work, the late nights, the early shifts. Each person looks at the pieces for which they were responsible: there is a great feeling of pride. Most of these people are part of the 'Home Team', those who never experience the glamour of motor racing in exotic locations: they don't even get to go to Silverstone for the testing. This is the closest many will get to the action, and it is a moment they savour.

Eventually Ron Dennis, the team's chief executive, also arrives to cast his eye over the car. But unlike the engineers and the other staff who are looking for imperfections or are just basking in the pride of their own work, Dennis is looking at the racing machine to see how he is going to 'dress' it. He has to place the all-important logos for the team's sponsors, all of whom have lengthy contracts with McLaren detailing to the millimetre where their name will figure on the car. Throughout the next couple of days – and nights – senior executives from Marlboro, Mercedes-Benz, Mobil and Boss will argue with Dennis over the positioning, and the size, of their logos. This ritual posturing is much loved by Dennis, who likes to negotiate over the minutiae of such matters. Yet this attention to detail, considered by many to border on the obsessive, is what makes the McLarens the best turned-out and most distinctive cars on the grid.

The introduction of the sponsors' logos at this late stage does not mean that this is some kind of afterthought. On the contrary, the quest for new backers, as well as the main-

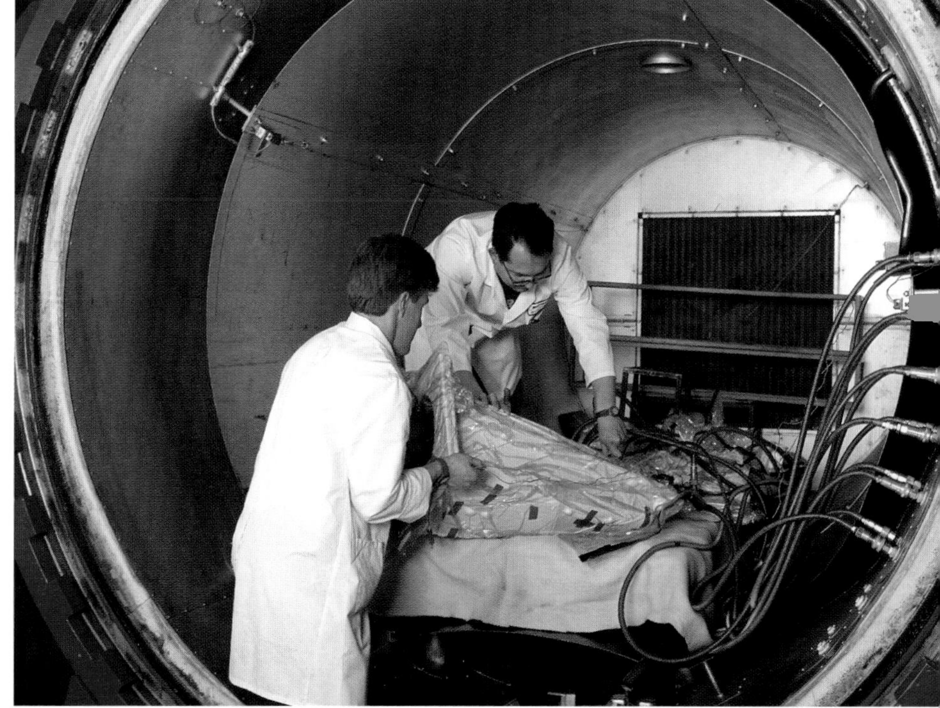

(opposite) The distinctive Marlboro red is sprayed on the finished parts alongside the remaining two kilos of paint which make up the car's distinctive livery.

taining of the existing ones is a full-time occupation for the marketing departments of all the teams. McLaren has been in the unusual position of having the rock-solid financial backing of Philip Morris, through its Marlboro brand, for the best part of 25 years. This eased the pressure of finding a big-name sponsor and allowed the team to focus primarily on the business of winning races. Only Ferrari has a similar lack of financial worries, while even Williams has had to change a huge number of sponsors in the past 20 years. Frank Williams often jokes that he learnt to speak French and Italian because that is where the sponsorship money was to be found.

McLaren may be on a sound financial footing, but it still hunts assiduously in order to bag enough backers to fill the spare parts of the car which have not been taken by Marlboro, or West, Philip Morris's successor. The company employs agencies and individuals in many countries to help identify likely prospects. These are then wooed, and invited to McLaren's headquarters in Woking where they are given a very sophisticated factory tour. In fact the word 'factory' is really a misnomer. From the moment prospective sponsors arrive in the reception area, with its World Championship-winning cars and its 330 back-lit trophies encased in glass, they'll know that this is no ordinary racing team, that indeed this is no ordinary sport. They will then be given an introductory talk by one of the marketing executives; will be shown films and sophisticated slide presentations in the luxury theatre; they will be walked around the workshops, all spotlessly clean, with white-coated staff silently going about their high-tech business. They will touch and hold carbon-fibre components, much lighter and much stronger than steel, they will be shown gearboxes, exhausts, steering wheels: they will be fully immersed

Henri Durand, McLaren's chief aerodynamicist, with the scaled down model of the 1996 McLaren being put through its paces in the wind tunnel.

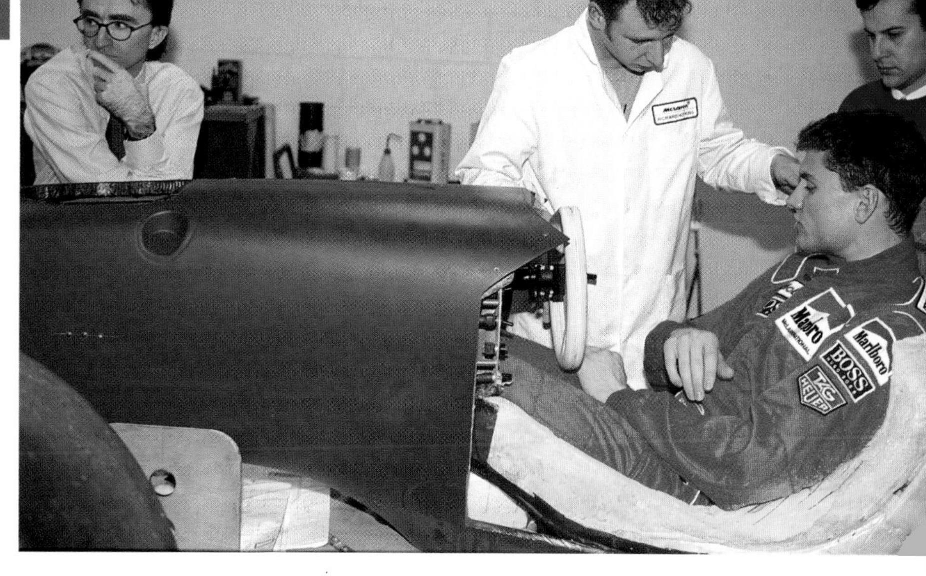

David Coulthard undergoing the lengthy fitting procedure where seat, chassis and pedals are tailored to the driver's body.

in the construction process of the car. Later, upstairs, in the grey-and-white offices where dozens of engineers and designers sit at immensely powerful computers, they will be shown, step by step, how some of the most intricate components are designed on the computer, the images revolving through 360 degrees as if suspended in space.

The target sponsor will then be treated to lunch in one of the three dining areas at McLaren. Usually it will be in the executive dining room, where they will be given fine wines, nouvelle cuisine and hear many more words of encouragement from the marketing people. If the prospective sponsor has indicated that a substantial sum of money may be available, Ron Dennis himself will put in an appearance. He comes in for coffee and takes over the lunch. A great salesman, he will do his high-octane seduction spiel, talking with great enthusiasm, regardless of who he is addressing. After he leaves, the guests are eased through the headquarters' glass doors and whisked away in a fleet of Mercedes estates towards Heathrow airport.

The quest for extra sponsorship is a never-ending one. But it is particularly frenzied over the winter months, when the attention of the marketing department can be focused more readily on this task as there isn't a Grand Prix every other week.

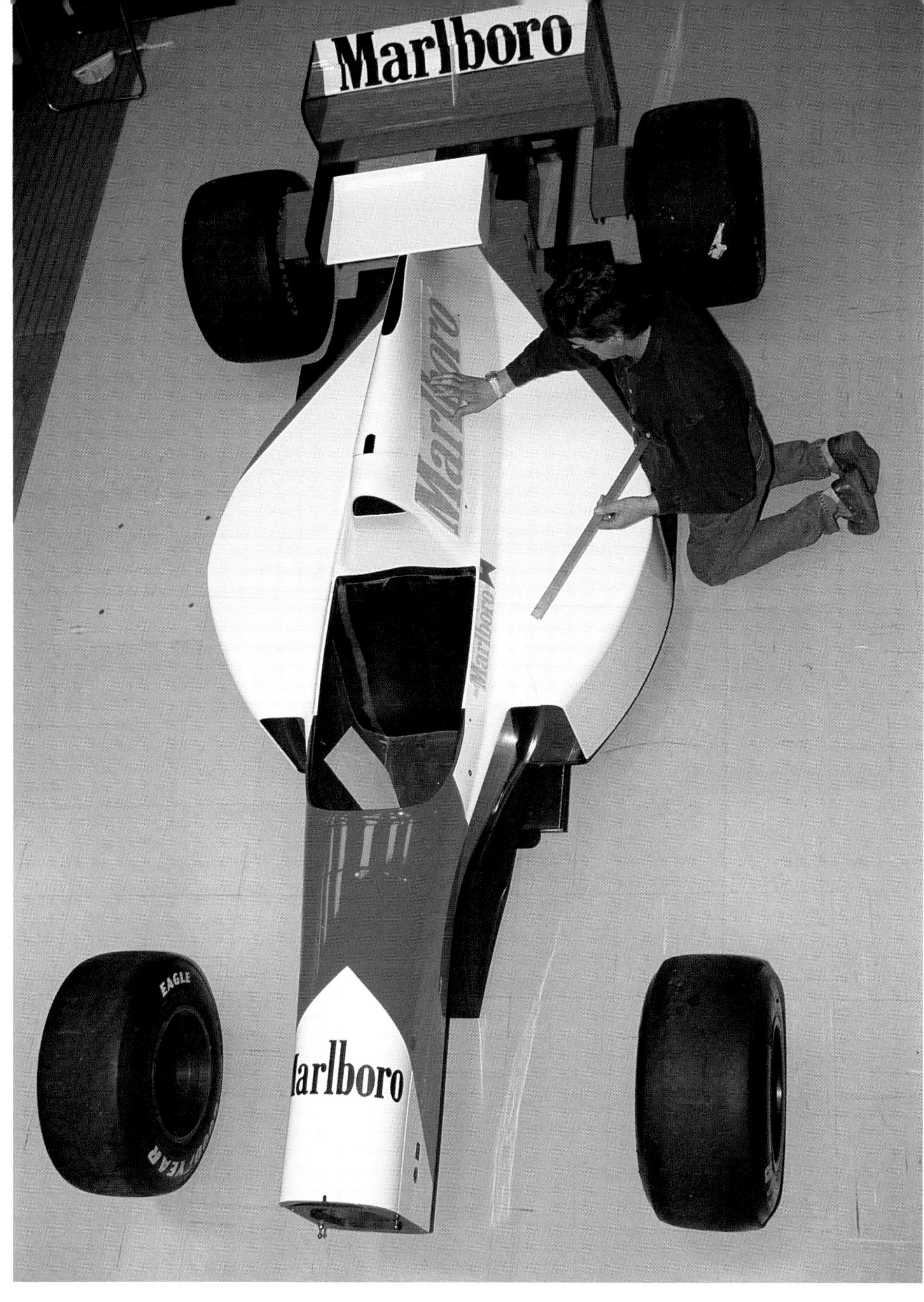

The positioning of the sponsor's logos is a crucial and integral part of the presentation of the new car.

When the new car finally has its first outing on track, it is the sum product of thousands of hours of work, in the workshop, the design office and in the marketing department. All these crucial elements in the team are honed to produce one thing only: the best possible car backed by the best possible financial security. The car is then delivered to the team manager and his race team: his task is to win races.

Anatomy of a Formula One Car Built by McLaren

Chassis

The chassis is the core feature of a racing car. It has to pass stringent FIA crash tests and it guarantees the safety of the driver.

It is created from composite material – layers of carbon fibre and aluminium honeycomb – and is five times lighter than steel but twice as strong. It weighs only 40 kilograms.

Fuel is stored in the chassis, behind the driver. It is made of two layers of very strong rubber (nitrile-buta-diene); the second layer is Kevlar reinforced to make it tear-resistant.

Each chassis carries an electronic transponder to show it has received FIA crash test approval. It can be read by race officials at each Grand Prix.

Transmission

McLaren uses a semi-automatic, six-speed gearbox which is designed and built in-house.

The gearbox casing, made of fully-stressed magnesium, holds both the engine and gearbox oils as well as carrying the rear suspension loads.

The carbon-fibre clutch is operated by a pair of levers on the steering wheel.

All of the gearbox functions are controlled by an on-board computer.

Each gear shift takes between 20 and 40 milliseconds.

Six gearboxes will be taken to each Grand Prix. There are up to 59 gear ratios available for each gearbox, thus the team may take up to 354 ratios to a race.

Race mechanics can change the six ratios in about 45 minutes.

Each transmission is rebuilt in the workshops after each race. Each gear is crack-tested and its mileage recorded.

Once used in a race, a ratio will not be taken to another Grand Prix, but, so long as it is sound, it will be used in testing.

Aerodynamics

The purpose of aerodynamics is to reduce the effect of drag in a straight line and to create downforce. This will result in higher straight line speed and better cornering performance.

Computer Aided Design (CAD) and Computational Fluid Dynamics (CFD) are used to simulate a variety of situations where aerodynamics play a fundamental role.

Much research is done in the wind tunnel. McLaren has adapted it to simulate track conditions through the use of a rolling road and moveable walls to follow the contours of the car.

Electronics

The complex electronics on a Formula One car require extensive wiring. On McLaren it amounts to about 1,000 metres.

There are more than 100 sensors, actuators and control units, all of them linked together.

Formula One is a very hostile environment for these fragile components: the vibrations and the G-forces on a car travelling at 320 kilometres per hour are very demanding. There is also much heat generated by the engine and the brakes.

Most software is designed either to improve the car's performance or to monitor it. The car is linked by data channels to the computers in the pits where the system engineers can intervene on the car, write new software, solve problems and interact with the driver and his race engineer.

Cooling

Unlike a road car, Formula One cars are cooled only when they move, thus there is no fan.

There are two side-mounted radiators.

The engine oil is cooled by a special radiator placed on the right-hand side of the car, while another is positioned above the gearbox to cool the oil in that component.

Bodywork

This is all built using carbon-fibre. It includes the engine cover, the nose cone, the wings, front suspension cover and the separate floor section.

The floor has a stepped base, to reduce adherence to the ground and therefore increase speed. It includes a wooden 'plank' made of Jabroc, normally used in racing yachts.

Set Up

In the last ten years the advent of telemetry has fundamentally changed the way a driver sets up a car. In fact, it has taken something away from the driver and increased the role played by the engineers, and in particular the race engineer.

Eddie Irvine wrestling with his Ferrari and showing why car balance is so crucial.

Phrases like, 'he drives by the seat of his pants', though still in use, have lost much of their meaning. Drivers still like to 'feel' the car as much as possible, to feel at one with it, but much of the work involved in making the car balanced, i.e. set-up, is now the task of the race engineer.

He is the man you see standing by the car, clipboard in hand, talking to the driver through the team's two-way radio system. Or you might see him on your television at the pit wall, a bank of computer screens in front of him, or he might be alongside the driver, both of them poring over sheets of telemetry data.

He will typically come from a team's drawing office, where he will have designed various aspects of the car. His job description is to put on track the most balanced and efficient racing car, in harmony with the driver,

parmalat

the circuit, the tyres and the weather conditions. As Tyrrell's Harvey Postlethwaite, the team's chief designer, put it, 'it is a 24-hour job, seven days a week, for the length of the racing season'.

It is not an easy task. Adjusting the minutiae of oversteer, ride heights, downforce and drag, often with changing weather conditions and the pressure of operating in a very competitive environment, both within the team and in the pit lane, requires a special kind of person, one who can cope with the fluidity of ever-changing truths. Added to this is the driver, who will have his own ideas about what has to be done. Thus the race engineer must also come equipped with a large dose of diplomatic skills, a grounding in the psychology of dealing with big egos and extremely broad, steady shoulders.

It is no wonder that the top race engineers are now in a position to command six-figure salaries from the big teams. In the past few years they have become ever more central to the effort of getting the best out of car and driver for the length of a race weekend. Despite all the electronics and the engineering, despite the telemetry and the reams of downloaded data, this is more than ever a 'black art'.

Before a Grand Prix weekend, the race engineer will be running simulated laps of the forthcoming circuit on his computer. He will be looking for the optimum balance in a variety of areas, but mostly he will be concentrating on the relationship between downforce and drag, oversteer and understeer, ride heights, fuel loads and tyre wear.

It is all to do with compromise. In the case of the downforce and drag relationship, it is clear that if an engineer is looking for more grip (downforce) he will increase the amount of wing, especially the rear one. This though, will slow the car down along the straights, as the engine has to pull along a great big barn door of wing. This, particularly for some of the smaller teams who do not have very powerful engines, would be a severe handicap. Thus the engineer has to search for the solution that will allow his car to grip in the corners and still have enough grunt down to the straights.

All of this is done at the team's headquarters in the days before a race. 'If you went to Tyrrell's drawing office on the Tuesday before a Grand Prix', says Postlethwaite, 'you'd see our engineers racing each other on the computer, to see who has the best race set-up. It's a bit of fun, but it's also pretty competitive.'

Another ingredient to be thrown into the pot is the fact that for many circuits the set-up for qualifying is not the one that will be used for the race. This applies to a circuit, for example, like the Hungaroring, where the unusual amount of wear on the left front tyre

Drivers still like to 'feel' the car ... but much of the work involved in making the car balanced is now the task of the race engineer.

The Hungaroring is particularly tough on tyres, and cars must be set up completely differently for qualifying and for racing.

(it will wear out after about 20 laps) makes a significant difference to the set-up required for the few laps in qualification and for the one that will take car and driver through one-and-a-half hours of racing, including the further variables brought in by the pit stops.

The race engineer will arrive at the track around midday on the Thursday before the

Minute adjustments are constantly being made on the cars throughout qualifying.

race. The cars will have been unloaded and rebuilt to the specifications set out by the race engineers. Engineer and driver will meet and discuss a few options for the following day and for the weekend. This is a pattern that is repeated in the next few days, with an early morning meeting followed by driving, followed by debriefing, more driving and finally a late afternoon meeting involving both drivers, the two race engineers, the team manager and other senior engineering personnel.

It is often the case that the race engineer, because of the driver's feedback or due to other changing factors, departs from the computer-induced set-up – which had been worked out at the factory – to a range of other ways of balancing the car. It is also often the case that come race day, the team will be reverting back to the original set-up. But at least this way, all the other solutions have been tried out 'for real'.

Most race engineers will feel that the computer simulation is still the best way to set up a car. They can dial in so many of the fixed reference points for each circuit – for example that you need traction in Monaco, and that the brakes will come under huge pressure in Canada – that the driver input is in many ways lessened. Engineers have the data from the previous year, they even have a record of the racing line and the braking points favoured by the driver. This is another way the race engineer can exert total control over the driver, and indeed the race team. His job is to make sure everything operates smoothly. He is the conductor of an orchestra.

today's top drivers still don't understand how to exploit the information from the telemetry. But Alain Prost, Ayrton Senna and now Michael Schumacher have always seen

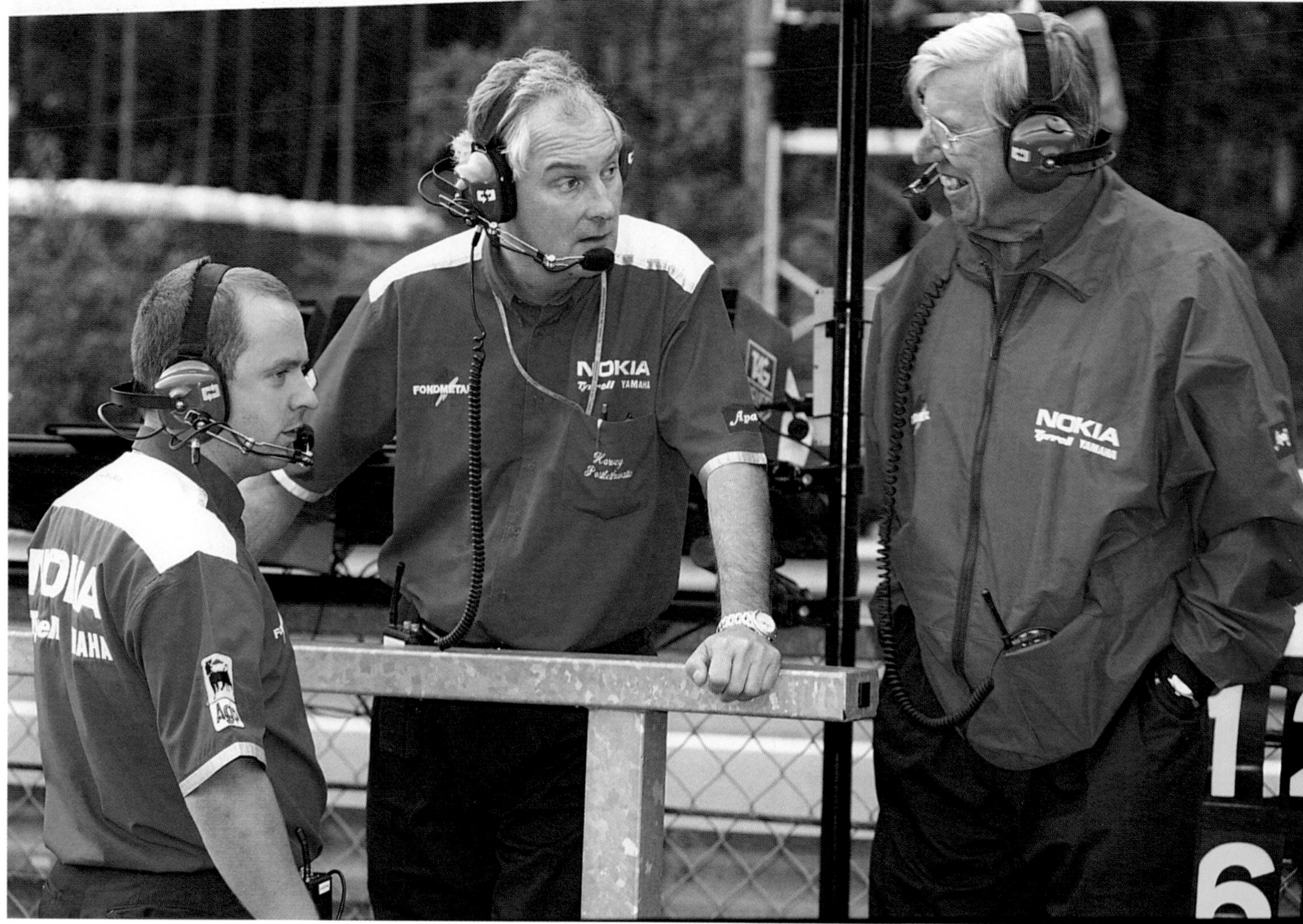

There is not much time to do all of this. Track time nowadays is very limited, so more of the analytical work is done in the engineering meetings, with the aid of the data from the telemetry. Drivers, on the whole, don't like this part of the business of racing. Gerhard Berger was famously scathing about the 'metres and metres of paper' he had to read during a race weekend. 'But the reality is that Ayrton Senna taught Gerhard how to use the telemetry to improve his driving,' says Postlethwaite. He says that some of

telemetry as another tool to help gain the advantage over the opposition.

Postlethwaite cautions that telemetry is not the magic wand for success in Formula One. 'Data still won't tell you everything about a car. It won't tell you, for example why a car is bad. You can overlay the telemetry traces of a good and a bad car: it won't give you the answers of why they perform differently.'

Clearly if telemetry was the crucial 'x' factor in a car's performance, then Ferrari and

Harvey Postlethwaite (middle) conferring with Ken Tyrrell (right) on the pit wall.

Marlboro
KENWOOD
Marlboro
BOSS
Sun
TENCEL
Sun

McLaren, the richest, most powerful teams, would always win. That, of course, is not the case. There is clearly more to it. Postlethwaite comes back to the analogy of

All data is fed into the pit lane computers for immediate evaluation.

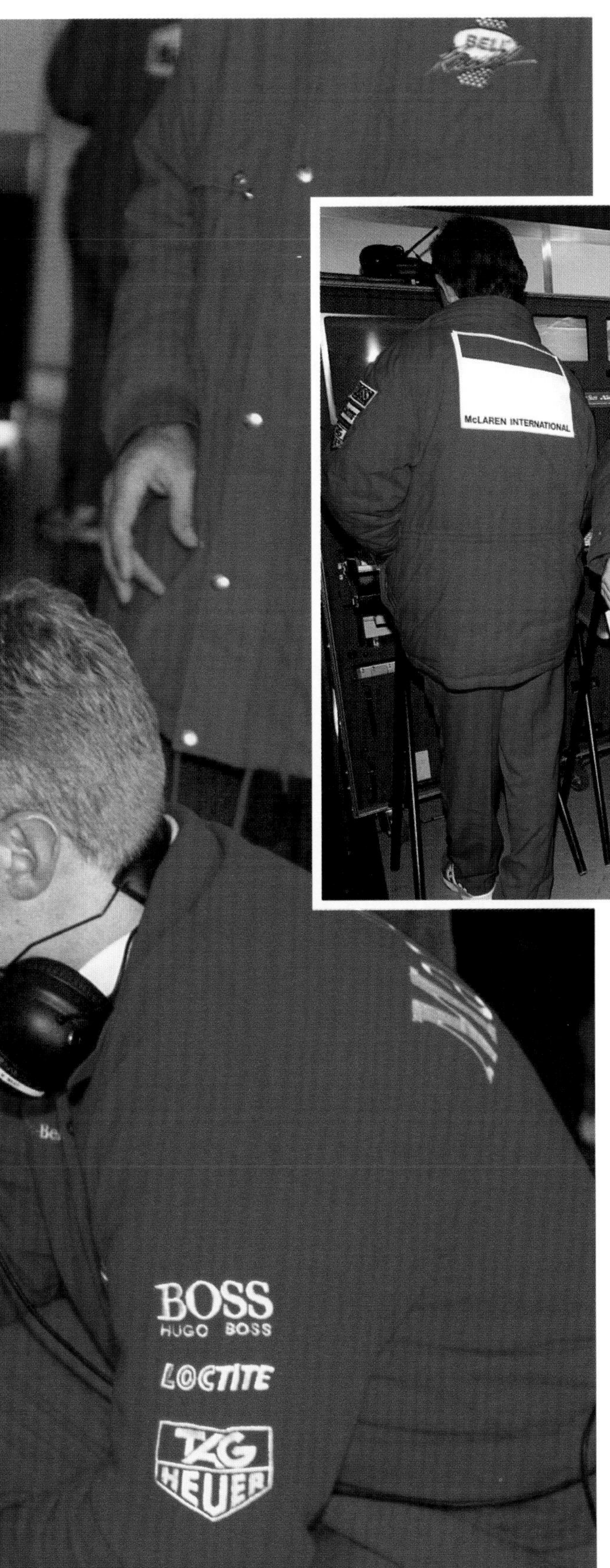

the orchestra conductor. 'Take a school orchestra. All the instruments are there, played competently by the musicians and led enthusiatically by the music master. The rhythm is there, the harmony, all is in place. But if you hear the same piece of music played by the Berlin Philarmonic conducted by, say, Claudio Abbado, it will be quite different.' The individuals, be they musicians or engineers, do make a difference. The human touch always does.

'Data will not help a slow driver go quicker,' says Postlethwaite. 'but a quick driver will go quicker if he understands how to exploit all this information.' All engineers have welcomed the amount of mechanical feedback telemetry makes available. All the temperatures are monitored for example. And there is no doubting the advances made

As soon as the drivers come in from a qualifying lap they are immediately debriefed by the engineers.

in Formula One racing that have come from aerodynamics and the use of composite fibres. Yet the science – or is it an art? – of data collection and analysis has not been perfected. Far from it.

In the days when the cars were even more complicated, some of the big teams' senior race engineers would still be at the track at 2am, hunched over their laptops, inputting massive amounts of data. At McLaren they worked in rotating groups of threes: one to work the keyboard, one to dictate, the other the check things over. They would often joke that in some races they had disappeared so far up their backsides, that they thought they'd never find the way out. The more data there was, the more obscure some of their set-up computer programmes would be.

One technique in vogue then, during the days of active suspensions, was 'fragmentation'. This involved dividing a corner in four sections, and then working out all of the best parameters for each of those sections. The aim was to have a car that changed gear, ride height and pitch automatically up to four times in each corner. No wonder the engineers were up till the early hours in the morning!

Though Grand Prix cars are much simpler now, the trend is still towards the power residing in the race engineer's hands, or more appropriately, mind. There are the exceptions. The aforementioned Prost, Senna and Schumacher, though still assigned top-of-the-

Ukyo Katayama assessing his own performance with the help of the computer's opinion.

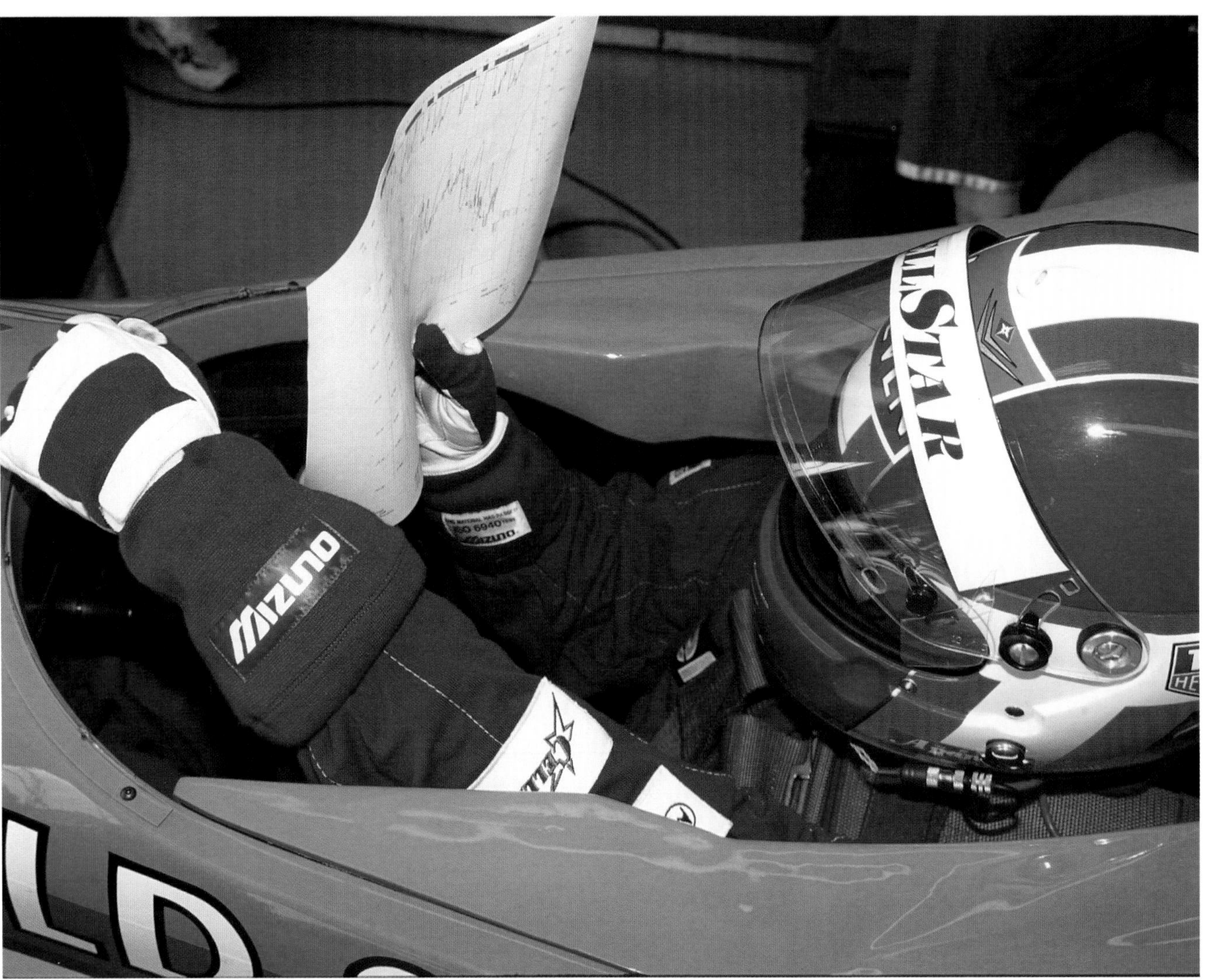

range race engineers, were and are able to contribute significantly to the set-up of their cars. To hear Senna begin quite literally to download information to his engineer as he was being pushed back into the pits after a qualifying lap was both an eye-opener and a privilege. No aspect of the car was left out, he spoke softly and impassionately and he had the respect of the engineers.

But he and Prost were unique. The next generation of drivers, barring Schumacher and possibly Damon Hill, are not in that league, and are consequently in the hands of their race engineers. Thus the trend is bound to favour the development of the engineering role. All the best race engineers will be able to combine scientific rigour with a little witchcraft. The drivers will be a little more like passengers of the team each season. Except for the great ones: they will shine through even more brightly and give great pleasure to racing fans.

The driver has plenty to think about in the cockpit.

Engine

Paul Morgan (left) and Mario Ilien, directors of Ilmor and makers of engines for Mercedes both in Formula One and Indy Car.

As you approach a Formula One circuit, especially if it is during one of the many test sessions the teams have throughout the year, when you're still about a mile away, you may be forgiven for thinking you've somehow strayed onto the set of Jurassic Park II. The reason for this is the primeval, muffled, yet incredibly loud high-pitched whine you are hearing. It seems to come closer, then it dies away again. It's like nothing you've ever heard before. It's frightening, but it also sends a tingle of excitement up your spine. Not that any of us would know what an angry, charging Tyrannosaurus Rex would sound like, but this, for my money, would be it.

As you approach the circuit, the noise gets louder and more discernible. You know, of course, it is an engine being put through its paces, screaming up to 17,000 rpms in sixth gear, then cutting down to a 50 mph corner, then back on the throttle again. It is deafening and exciting. It may not be from a dinosaur – Formula One designers would very much resent their jewels being called that – but the primeval, gut-wrenching sound is straight out of another world, one that is within us. The noise unlocks it, and the excitement mounts.

Ordinary fans, with no apparent grounding in mechanical engineering, can be heard talking of the unmistakable sweetness of the Ferrari V12, of the driveability of the Renault, of the top speed of the Peugeot. Engine designers have become household names. Renault's Bernard Dudot's craggy face adorns many of the interviews he gives to the press; Osamu Goto, the man behind the legendary Honda power which did so much for McLaren, has for the past few years done the rounds of the top teams, head hunted in turn by McLaren, Ferrari and Ford. You can be sure that he is not short of a bob or two. Mario Ilien, co-owner of Ilmore, bespoke providers of engines to Mercedes' racing efforts in Indy and in Formula One, is a familiar figure around the circuits, as is Brian Hart, the last of the great British artisan engine makers, who with no budget turns out quite wonderful power units.

An engine deal is the first thing a constructor wants. You can design the greatest car, have the best driver, but if you don't have the grunt, you''ll go nowhere fast. When Eddie Jordan came into Formula One, he managed to secure a deal with Ford. That made all the difference: his first season was a good one for a newcomer. Jackie Stewart has made it a pre-condition for his entry in Formula One to have a works Ford engine in the back of his car. Flavio Briatore, head of Benetton Formula but also owner of Ligier, spent a great deal of the 1996 season sparring with Tom Walkinshaw, his former partner, who was trying to wrestle away the Mugen-Honda engine from Ligier for his new Arrows team in 1997.

Broadly speaking there are four kinds of engine deals a Formula One team can have. The first is the all-singing, all-dancing partnership. This means that the engine manufacturer will do whatever is necessary to make the relationship a successful one. It will invest huge resources in R & D, as well as providing extensive backup, both financially and in manpower. The engine manufacturer will also be hands-on when it comes to decision-making, be it about race strategy, choice of drivers or aspects of the car design that touch on the engine, such as radiators. All constructors want this kind of deal. It is the best route to success. But it does have its drawbacks. Fiercely independent constructors don't usually take kindly to being told what to do by large corporations. The pressure can be huge and the resulting friction will cause sparks to fly. It is due to the skill of the top constructors that they manage to

One of the many computerized robots essential to the manufacture of Formula One engines.

make it all work throughout a long and fraught season. These are the kind of deals Williams and Benetton have with Renault and McLaren with Mercedes.

There is another level, and that is where the engine manufacturer still has a works deal with team, but the amount of support is less, though in real financial or technical terms the amount of input is equal to Renault or Mercedes. For example, Peugeot has made a huge effort to bring its engine up to a level to match Renault. By all accounts they have done a very good job, but they have not helped Jordan in parallel to their own effort. Thus Jordan is still having to seek sponsorship wherever it can find it and the French engine manufacturer will not dig into its pockets to help the Silverstone-based team. Sauber's Ford deal is set up along similar lines.

Then there is the mass of the remaining teams which have a variety of deals, some quite hard to unravel. Essentially, though, it all comes down to the fact that they have to pay for their engines. Prices vary, but figures will not be too far off the $5m–$8m mark yearly. That is a lot of money for a team operating at the middle of the grid: it could amount to a third, if not a half, of its yearly budget.

Finally there is the Ferrari way of doing things. This is the only team which builds its own car and engine. It requires a massive effort, one that the other constructors and engine manufacturers consider too big. Formula One, they argue, is becoming ever more technical and specialized. By separating the engine build from the car build, a team will get the best out of both.

Ferrari do not agree with this, pointing out that theirs is the most challenging and the purest way to go motor racing. Yet, in recent years they have recognized that their weakness lay in the design and the use of advanced composite fibres and have set up a design centre in England under the direction of John Barnard. Their engine-making ability is instead their pride and joy. So, in their

High precision cutting techniques are used to manufacture Mercedes race engines.

own way, they have tacitly gone along with the prevailing opinions in Formula One by separating their car construction operation from that of engine building.

There is always much discussion about which engine is more powerful, the fastest, how much horsepower, how many rpms. Most of the engine gurus scoff at these questions, pointing out that an engine is not an isolated unit within a car, but part of a package made up of chassis, gearbox, aerodynamic factors, cooling system and suspension. It is also influenced by fuel and oil, the circuits, the weather and the driver's individual style.

At every race Tag-Heuer, the official timekeepers, produce much data for the teams covering a wide range of speed and timing information. Thus all teams will know exactly what the top speeds are, how fast the cars are exiting corners and so on. But again, the straight line speed of a Grand Prix car is also related to the aerodynamic configuration. Thus, if the car is not very grippy, it will carry a lot of wing to get it safely and quickly around the corners. This, though, will slow it down on the straights, hiding the true top speed of the engine.

At Silverstone this year the fastest car (in terms of straight-line speed) was Martin Brundle's Jordan-Peugeot, as he crossed the start-finish line, during qualifying, at 177.5 mph. Second and third fastest were the McLaren-Mercedes and fourth fastest was the other Jordan-Peugeot. The Williams-Renault were respectively 10th and 12th fastest, with Damon Hill clocking 172.9 mph. But Hill ended up on pole, his teammate Jacques Villeneuve was alongside him and Martin Brundle was in eighth place, more than two seconds adrift from Hill.

The Mercedes V-10 engine in all its glory.

What this tells us is that the big grunt engines in the Jordan and McLaren cars could not overcome the inadequacies, at least on this circuit, of their car and driver combination. The supremely balanced Williams could afford not to have to draw more than was needed from the Renault engine in order to qualify both drivers on the first row of the grid.

The mind goes back to Nigel Mansell in the McLaren in 1995. As far as he was concerned, the fact that the car was not predictable in the way he wanted, made the power of the engine irrelevant. It was the same for Martin Brundle in the Jordan this year. Great speed in the engine, but a car he did not feel comfortable with and one that he could therefore not push in the corners as much as he would have liked. Driver confidence in the car's handling is paramount. And if on top of an unsettled car there is an engine that lacks driveability – providing a smooth power curve, especially when exiting corners – then the driver really has a beast in his hands, one that may be very hard to tame.

Ayrton Senna would very often talk of the 'package', meaning all of the components, including the driver, which makes up a successful Grand Prix car. In his days at McLaren, it was felt by many, including the Brazilian ace, that the supreme Japanese engine made up for the deficiencies of the McLaren chassis. He could have added, though he never did, that his driving made a hell of a difference too. Of the three main components of the package – the engine, the car and the driver – at least two need to be very good and able to work in harmony. In Senna's days at McLaren, it was the engine and the driver. For Michael Schumacher at Benetton, it was the driver and the car one year; then, as Benetton became the second team to be supplied with with the Renault V10, it was all three in 1995. For Williams, it was car and engine in 1995, while Hill's big improvements in 1996 made it the perfect triangle of car, engine and driver for 1996.

When the three components are all working in harmony, the combination is near unbeatable. Except for the challenge from one's own team mate. That is a rare occurence but we had a taste of it from Villeneuve in 1996.

The announced withdrawal of Renault from Formula One racing will cause a huge shift in the power stakes. Peugeot, Mercedes and possibly Mugen-Honda will be the engines to have. Ford might have to increase its commitment and Ferrari will, as ever, be prey to the vagaries of their internal politics. It will make for exciting racing in 1998.

A Formula One engine is a remarkably compact and lightweight example of state of the art engineering.

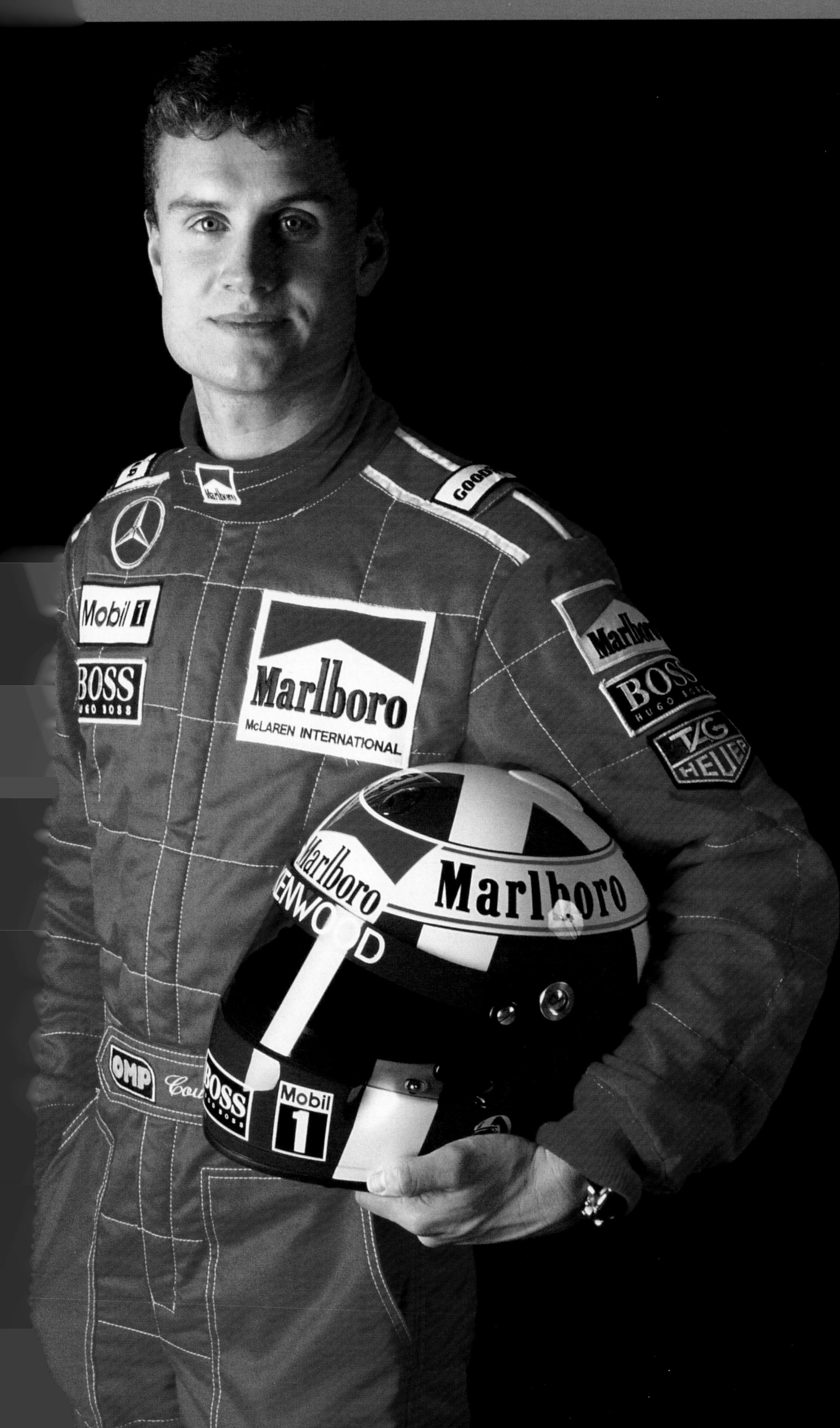
Mobil 1
BOSS
HUGO BOSS
Marlboro
McLAREN INTERNATIONAL
Marlboro
Marlboro
Marlboro
OMP
BOSS
Mobil
1

Fitness

On the face of it, it doesn't look much like a sport. No one is kicking a ball and chasing after it, no one is running till their lungs feel like bursting, no massive weights are lifted and no one is shuffling around a ring hitting an opponent as hard as possible.

Formula One drivers don't really look much as we expect sportsmen to as they wander around the paddock languidly resplendent in their multicoloured overalls, tanned, good-looking, heading for their motor homes, where they are fed, massaged and cosseted before getting into a car and driving around for less than a couple of hours. Nice work if you can get it. And the money? Well, there are barrel-loads of it.

There is, however, another way of seeing this. Squeeze yourself into an opening that is narrower than your shoulders, strap yourself in so tight that you can hardly breathe. Put a helmet on, realize that you can't see much, except for straight ahead. The engine roars to life. You engage first gear, slowly move out of the garage. At the end of the pit lane, still going at a modest 120 kph, you hit the smallest of bumps: you feel as if you've been dropped on it bum first, wearing only your underpants. The jolt is magnified through the bottom of the spine, up your back and is felt most strongly in your neck. You go down the straight, up the gears to sixth, approach the first corner and slow down to fourth. As you do this you have to push really hard with your right leg on the brake pedal. You hold your breath. The car shudders, and you feel as if you've been hit on the back of the head with a sledgehammer. Then you wrestle the car round the bend, your head wanting to go the other way, your neck muscles straining to breaking point, your legs flapping around. As you hit the apex you start squeezing the throttle, your arms still straining on the steering wheel, your back and neck muscles taut. Then you're on the straight, breathing again, heart rate dropping to 140 beats per minute from around 180-190 beats per minute. Up comes the next bend. Another sledgehammer blow to the back of the head, and so on, maybe 200 or 300 times in a race.

Grand Prix racing is tough. It's either very hot – in Hungary in August the ambient temperature is often 40 degrees centigrade – or so wet that there is quite literally no visibility. Drivers must be able to cope with tension and pressure. Their reflexes must be pin-sharp, their decision-making faultless. They must have excellent cardiovascular capability as well as strength and stamina. So yes, it is nice work, but it is also hard work. And you have to like pain, fear, cramp, heat and dehydration. And the money, it's definitely good. But one small mistake, and all your riches become irrelevant.

Formula One racing drivers have to be athletes. David Coulthard is part of a generation of drivers for whom fitness and total commitment to their chosen sport is second nature. From his earliest karting days, his father constantly reminded him that he had to be fit, that he had to be stronger than all the others. This notion is deeply rooted in

David Coulthard, trim-looking, though not apparently overly athletic.

The cramped and narrow cockpit is a tough working environment.

the young Scottish driver, who has always trained. 'I used to go swimming every day. All the sport I did was aimed at driving. At Williams, even when I was a test driver, I went to the gym three times a week.'

Leberer learned his trade at an unusual health clinic in the Austrian Alps. This is where Niki Lauda went after his horrific accident at the old Nürburgring and where Gerhard Berger also went after his accident

Now he has Josef Leberer alongside him. Many believe the diminutive Austrian is the best trainer in Formula One. Ayrton Senna did, and he asked Leberer to move with him to Williams when the Brazilian ace left McLaren. The Austrian is now back at McLaren, where he looks after Coulthard, Mika Hakkinen and Jan Magnussen, the test driver.

at Imola in 1989. Traditional medicine takes a back seat here, while complementary medicine is instead very much to the fore. Oriental and Western medical philosophies are mixed in a cocktail of herbs, juices, vitamins and root extracts. The patients (though many of the sportsmen who go there like to think of themselves as victims) are subjected to all kinds of manipulation, massage and hydrotherapy. The gym work is tough, and the standard of the runs and bike rides in the mountains is not for the faint-hearted.

A semi-professional footballer who had to retire after a knee injury, Leberer is as interested in the mental side of sport as he is in the physical. His central belief is that a fit driver is a confident driver. In his opinion lesser drivers are always on the look-out for excuses, which worked up until quite recently. But now the teams have so much electronic feedback from the cars, there is no hiding behind 'the car just slid away from me' type of excuse. If it did, more often than not it will be a driver error. And as far as Leberer is concerned, mistakes are made by unfit drivers. 'A driver must be able to deal with the tension, the pressure of driving a Grand Prix car in such a demanding environment. He must also be able to keep his level of performance at an optimum level, despite the challenges of others, despite the expectations of the team, and despite the attention of the media.' This is the difference between the top drivers and the rest of the field: the way they handle pressure.

The basis of understanding the physical fitness requirements for a Grand Prix driver rests on two closely linked premises. Firstly, drivers are sportsmen who 'play' their game squeezed tightly into a very confined space: there is hardly any room to move. Secondly all drivers want to 'feel' the car. Senna often used to say: 'I must feel the car'. Four times a world champion, the Brazilian had an extraordinary relationship with his car: he felt everything, he saw everything, he heard everything – he was part of the machine.

To do this he strapped himself in so tightly that he'd be near collapse at the end of some races. Even without going to his extremes, all drivers do nevertheless ply their trade tightly strapped into a very confined space. Because of the driving position, and because the car has no suspension to speak of, all the strain is in the neck: it has to absorb both the lateral and longitudinal G-forces, when the head and helmet can end up weighing four times their original weight, as well as the vertical ones caused by hitting

The driver's body is subjected to a lateral pull of up to 4 G when negotiating corners. Most of the strain is felt on the neck.

bumps at high speed. The worst pain often comes when a driver exits out of a long, fast corner and hits a bump. Driver and car take off and are airborne. The body instinctively relaxes, but when it comes down violently, the shock is awesome. It travels from the base of the spine to the neck. Always a very sensitive area, the neck and all its delicate bones, muscles and nerves come under terrible pressure.

Though drivers do undergo a range of special exercises to strengthen their necks, overall fitness is very important. Leberer trains his drivers so that they have stamina, power and strength. Above all, especially in the brief off-season, he works on increasing the cardiovascular endurance. Senna paid particular attention to his heart and lung capacity: already some years ago he would go on long runs with a heart-rate monitor strapped to his chest, a sure sign of the importance he attributed to this side of his fitness.

At the start of a race, and for the first few bends, the heart can be pumping uncomfortably close to its maximum of 200-220 beats per minute. Throughout the race it stays higher than most of us have ever experienced; at any time during the two-hour period a driver is competing in a Grand Prix, it

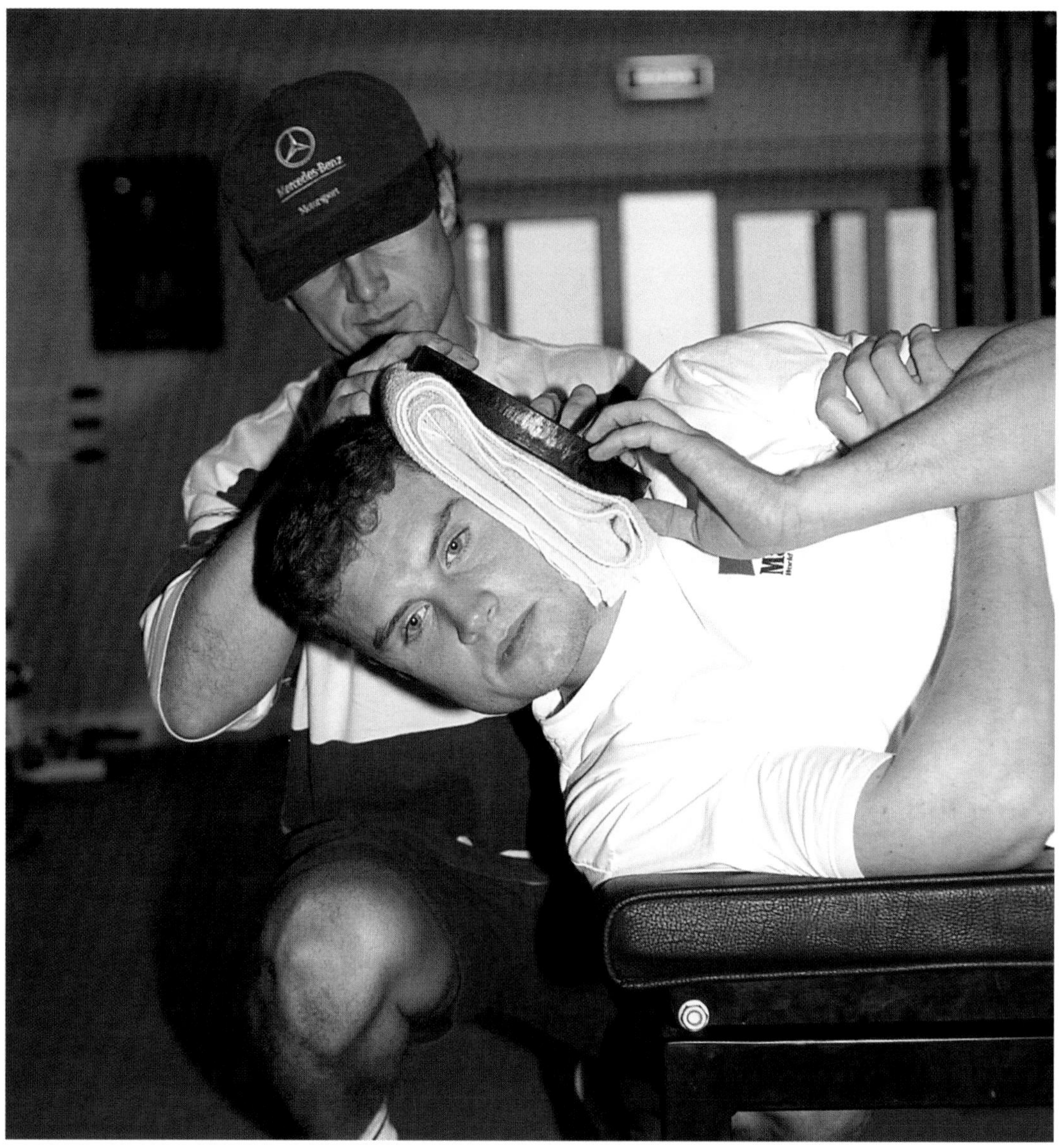

Joseph Leberer, McLaren's fitness expert, subjects David Coulthard's neck to some unusual exercises.

can shoot right up again, caused by an accident, a sudden avoidance or a brake failure.

Top drivers have the resting heart rate of a long-distance runner. Yet they never move, at least not in the conventional sense. Their legs have to be very strong, the fast twitch muscles must be highly developed because reaction time is very important. A driver must be able to squeeze the throttle lightly, the brakes hard, and at times the speed at which his feet move in the narrow confines of the chassis is mesmerizing: a mixture of soft, feathery touches and of hard-hitting stomping and stabbing.

The other area drivers need to develop is the upper back and the arms. Leberer feels that most of the drivers he has worked with were in good shape in terms of the muscles they needed to drive a Grand Prix car. He has, admittedly, worked with some of the best, while at McLaren and at Williams, but he feels that most Formula One drivers have developed the right muscles for the job. The problem is that the hours spent in the car using only very specific muscles have often altered their posture – usually a slight hunch forwards with the shoulders rolled inwards – a sure sign that the opposite muscles have been insufficiently developed. Leberer has his drivers exercise many muscles which they

Strong leg muscles are extremely important to help the driver both brace himself in the cockpit and to apply the necessary pressure on the brake.

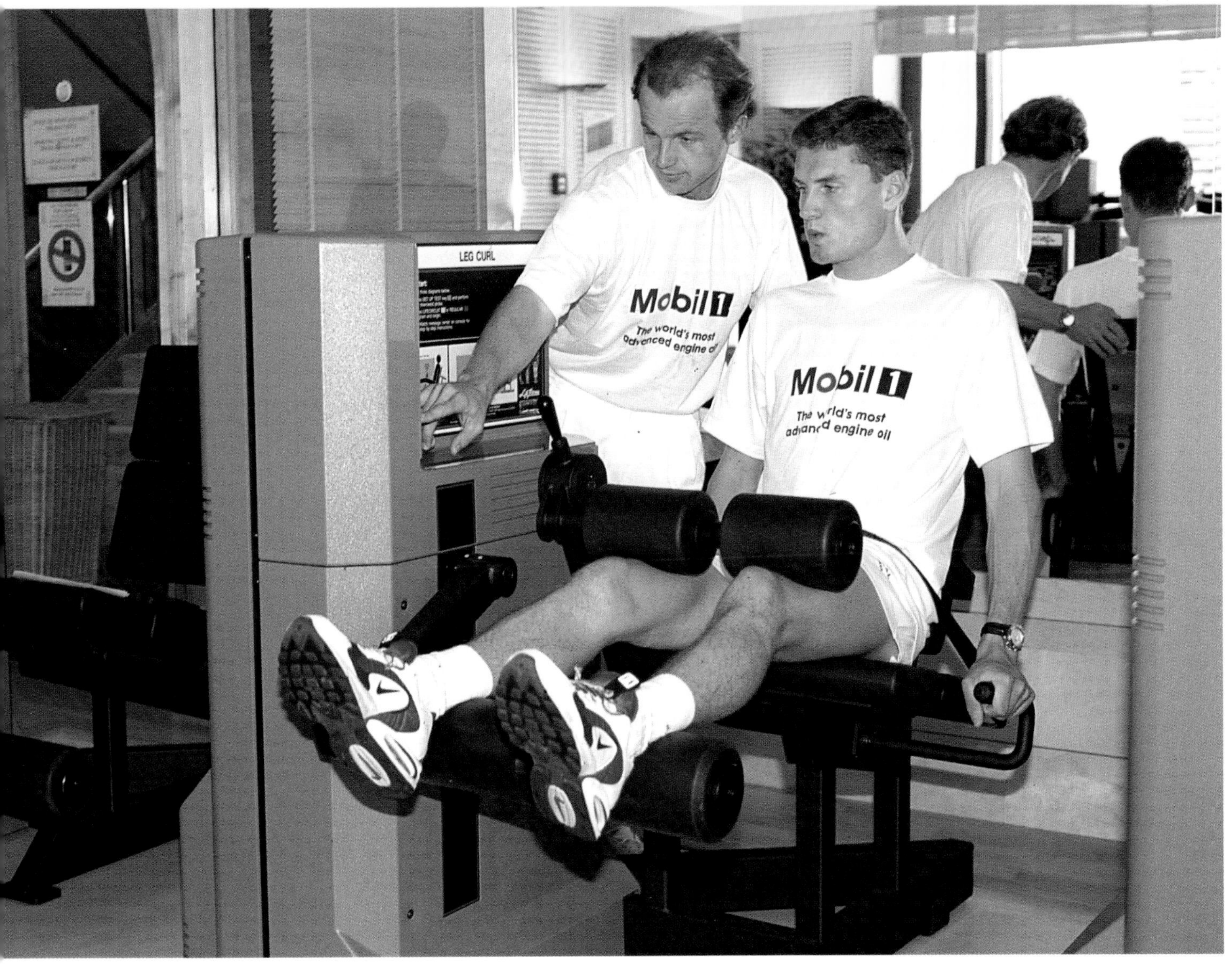

don't use for driving. 'But the importance of these muscles is that, by working in opposition, they will make the driving ones work

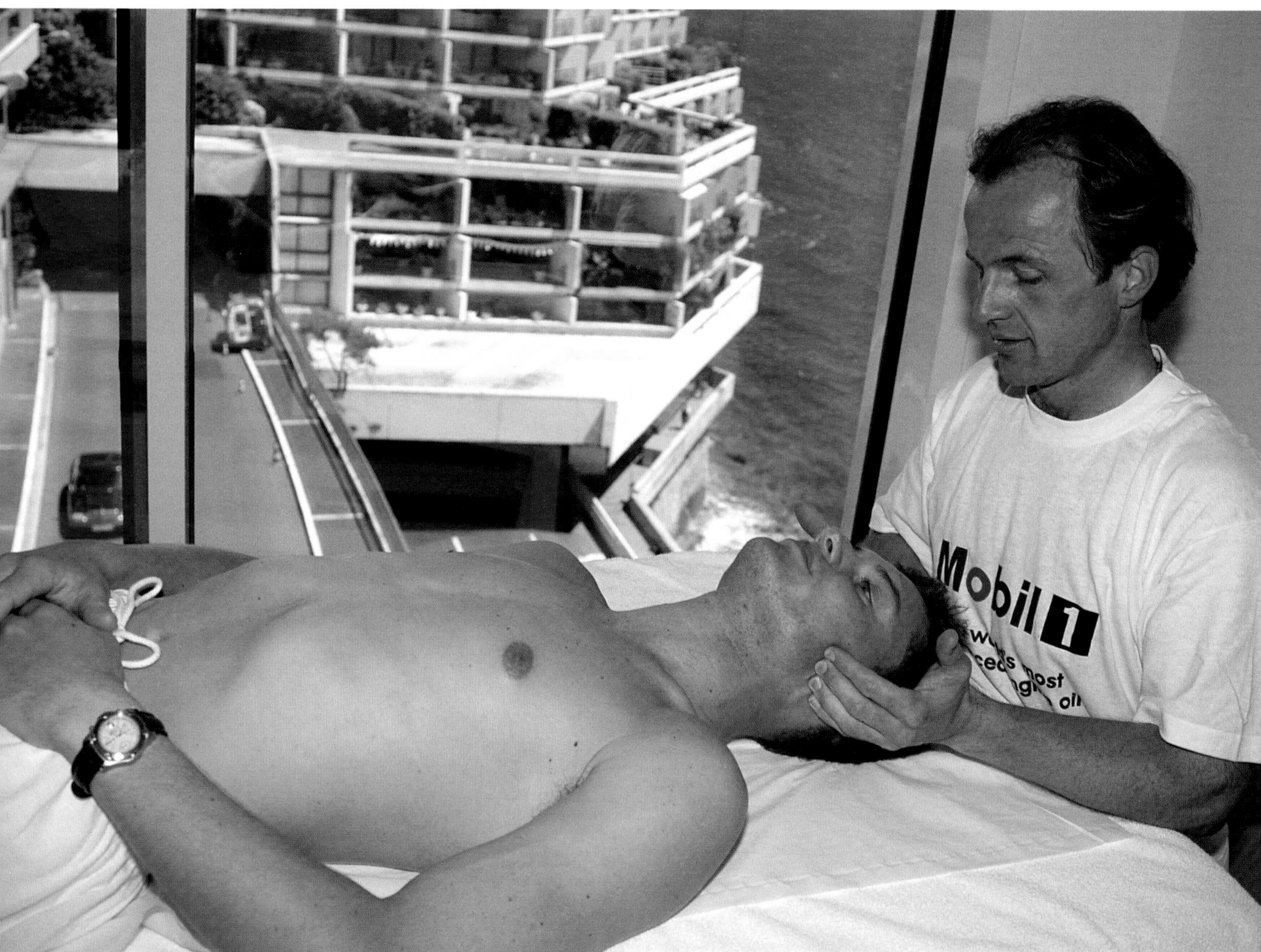

better and faster.'

Coulthard feels he has benefitted from having Leberer in the team. He had seen how Leberer worked when the Austrian was at Williams in 1994, looking after Senna, and the Scotsman was the test driver. After that, he admits that the trainers he had were only there to keep him topped up at the races. But last winter he spent a lot of time with Leberer in Austria, cross-country skiing and learning a whole series of conditioning and stretching exercises. Coulthard has long had a lower back problem, the result of a karting accident, and the two worked on ways of rectifying it. This sort of attention to detail helps build up the relationship between driver and trainer, one that becomes as close and as important as the one that develops between the driver and his race engineer.

Contrary to popular belief, drivers lead very full lives. During a race weekend they will spend much time glad-handing sponsors and their guests. After the race, the Monday should be spent recuperating – it takes about two days to shake the rigours of a race out of the system – but the day after the British Grand Prix, Coulthard was playing 18 holes of golf in aid of charity. Then he was off to an evening function, and so on, and so on.

In the middle of this tornado of engagements, media calls, charity dinners, business meetings, test sessions and Grand Prix weekends, the driver has to keep part of himself focused on the job he is paid to do. Leberer encourages his charges to cross-train as much as possible, trying different sports, so as to keep their enthusiasm for exercise alive throughout the long season and the time zone changes. This is part of the mental training through which he also puts the drivers. Visualization has now become a clichéd word in sporting circles, but racing drivers have been doing it for a very long time, before sport psychologists made it into a fashion accessory for any cool and media-aware sportsperson.

Ayrton Senna attracted undeserved ridicule when he tried to explain to a disbelieving motor-racing media that he could actually 'see' two bends ahead, and that he had trained himself to drive that way. Stung by facile quips about 'having God on his side', the Brazilian clammed up and very rarely spoke in public about this aspect of Grand Prix driving. But when I asked him about it, and once he had ascertained that I was genuinely interested in this subject, Senna spoke at huge length about the mental side of driving, the relationship with fear, with the car, with the track. It was quite obvious that over and above an amazing aptitude for driving a racing car very fast, he also had trained himself to be as fit and as

Relaxation and visualisation techniques are an important factor in a Formula One driver's mental fitness.

sharp in his mind as he was in his body.

It is no coincidence that Leberer was already working with him at McLaren at the time. The respect they had for each other was palpable and they clearly learned much together. The Austrian is adamant that the mental side is crucial. It is a question of attitude. Visualizing what lies ahead, that is seeing in the mind's eye, is the 'x' factor which can make the difference in a sport where hundredths of a second count. The end product of visualization is that a driver must be able to react positively and winningly to any situation that he faces, because he has already encountered this situation in his mind and decided how to deal with it. There are no hesitations. It is the ultimate automatic pilot using the right and left sides of the brain. The focus of this training is to minimize mistakes and maximize the positive.

All of this can be tough for drivers who have come to Formula One with no more than a very large right foot lubricated by free-flowing testosterone. Speed is the most important attribute for a racing driver. But what propelled them through the lower formulae does not cut much of a swathe in Grand Prix racing. Witness the scores of Formula 3000 championship winners who have floundered and disappeared from the Formula One scene, after wrestling underachieving cars headed for nowhere around the world's toughest circuits.

The driver must combine physical and mental strength in order to cope with the variety of tasks he is faced with over a race weekend.

The extra factor that singles out fast drivers is how they use their head. Leberer concedes that teaching this side of the craft of racing cars can be an uphill task. Already under pressure from the race engineers to practically outperform the trackside computers when feeding data back to the technical staff in the pits, some drivers will struggle to accept that they have to learn one more time-consuming skill. 'When they have been doing things for 15 to 20 years, they are reluctant to change. But it is good to do different things, and they have to trust me.'

Drivers also have to trust Leberer with what they eat. The Austrian shares the tiny kitchens in the motor homes with a very busy team of young ladies who are charged with the catering arrangements for the whole of the McLaren team. Weaving in and out of the controlled lunchtime mayhem after practice and before races, he appears next to the driver with a small dish of pasta, or white meat, fresh vegetables and fruit. In the morning he will be up at dawn to prepare the muesli from grains selected and mixed by him. He is aware of allergies, likes and dislikes. Everything that is eaten is geared to enhance the driver's performance. Indeed everything the drivers put in their body must be geared towards producing more energy and more power.

For this reason Leberer is very reluctant to use medicines of any kind, even vitamins. He is convinced that it is a process of education, of trust. 'If the drivers know why they are doing it, why they are eating some foods as opposed to others, they will continue to do so when I'm not around. Their confidence increases too. With Ayrton we never used drugs. If there was a problem, we always looked for ways of solving it without medicines. Of course you can't do this with any driver. Some are special, others are quite useless.'

Though tyres, and tyre wear, are important, what influences the pit stops is the refueling process.

In Formula One, the correct race strategy can make a huge difference between a finish in the points and one outside the scoring positions. For the top teams, it can make the difference between a win and a runner-up place. In the most extreme cases, it can deliver a win to a team which, on past form, should be nowhere near a podium finish.

This is what happened to Ligier at the 1996 Monaco Grand Prix. Through a succession of big name retirements, and a quick re-appraisal of its race strategy, the French team found itself vying for first place with mighty McLaren. Of the two outfits, it was the French who thought quickest on their feet and left David Coulthard behind in second place. It was their pit stop strategy which won them the race. Conversely, it was McLaren's apparent inability to change their game plan that denied the the much longed-for first victory after Ayrton Senna's last in Adelaide in 1993.

Since the introduction of refuelling three years ago, Formula One racing has changed. The trend towards narrow, twisty circuits had led to a paucity of excitement: it was so hard to overtake, that whoever was on pole, barring mechanical or electronic problems, was likely to win the race. Partly in response to this, Bernie Ecclestone proposed the re-introduction of refuelling. I say partly, because the other reason was the alleged desire to help Ferrari: a strong 'prancing horse' is good for Formula One, and its V12 engine had become so thirsty that it struggled to make it through some of the races. Thus refuelling was brought back in.

Privately, the teams were adamantly opposed to this. In the first place because of the 'Ferrari' factor, and in the second place because of the danger which refuelling would bring to the pit lane. 'An accident waiting to happen', is how Ron Dennis described the situation. Many of the mechanics were also concerned, especially when the refuelling rigs supplied by the FIA turned out to be less than fool proof. The horrendous pit lane fire which engulfed Jos Verstappen and his Benetton mechanics might have been the last straw in the debate which had been raging behind closed doors. Surely there would be a concerted move to ban refuelling.

Instead, many of the teams had come to realize the importance of dialling more variables into the course of a Grand Prix. Especially the smaller and less financially powerful ones were quick to find advantages. For example, Tyrrell's Mika Salo is good at overtaking, but in the Yamaha he does not have the most powerful engine in the pit lane. Thus Tyrrell have devised a race strategy which involves a relatively high number of pit stops. This means the Finnish driver is carrying a light load and can at least hope to overtake more powerful cars which are carrying more fuel, and are therefore heavier.

Many of the engineers in the pit lane think it has taken three years for the teams to

Race Strategy

The pit wall is the command centre where all strategic decisions are taken in the course of a Grand Prix.

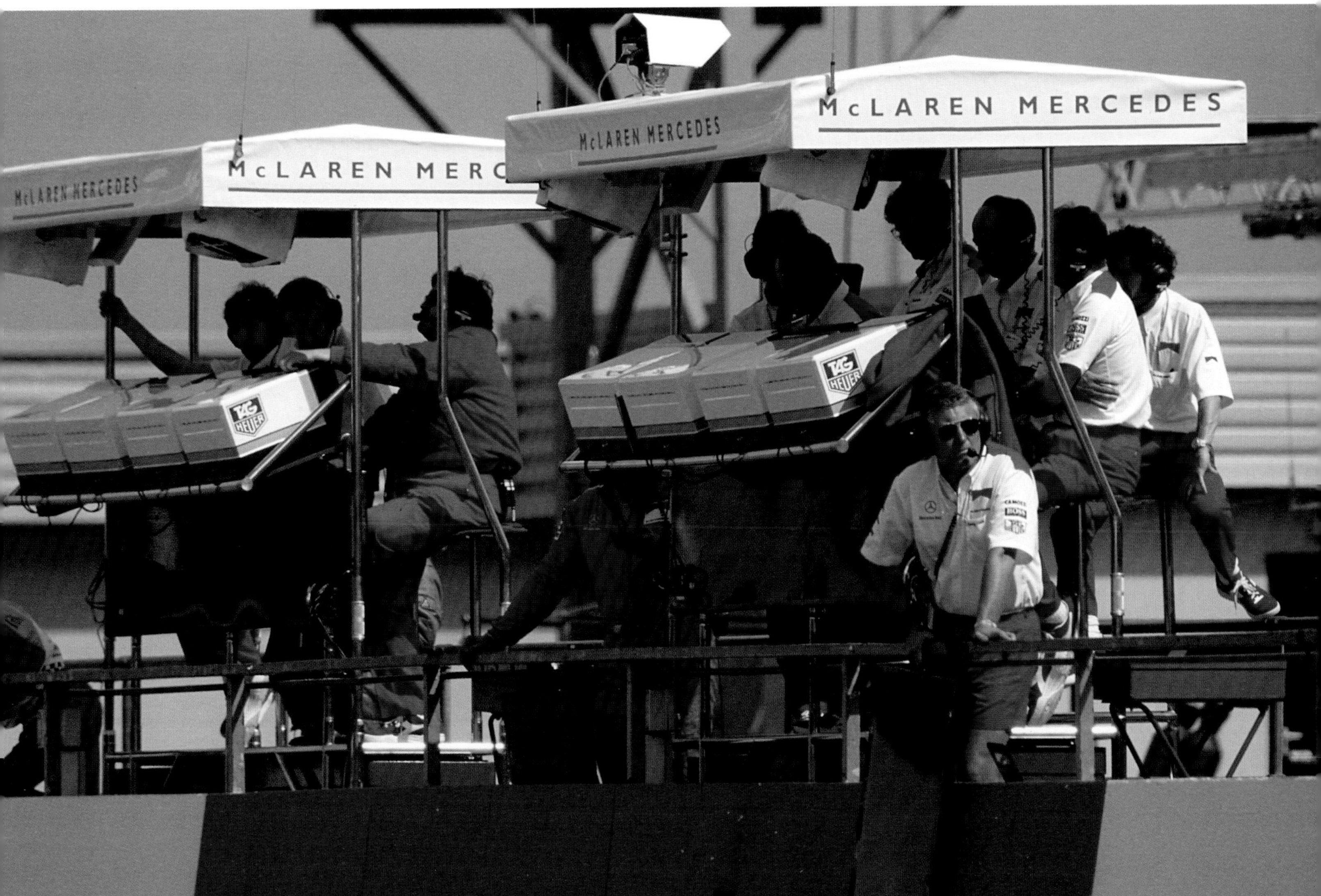

come to terms with the subtleties, and the possibilties, of the new-style pit stop. Once more, it all starts with computer simulation. Factors like the length of the pit lane are taken into consideration, as are the average times it takes to enter, refuel and then exit. The Hungaroring is tough on tyres, so one might as well run a three-stop strategy. This will lead to a lighter car and less wear on the tyres. The pit lane in Germany is very long, thus much time would be wasted by entering it more times than is strictly necessary. It is the same for Silverstone, so for both these races, most of the teams will go for a one-stop race strategy.

Though tyres, and tyre wear, are important, what influences the pit stops is the refuelling process. Most teams have become so good at tyre changes that they will perform their magic in around five seconds. In that time they will also load about 50 litres of fuel. That time, give or take a second, will be in line for a three-stop strategy. If instead the first stop is about seven or eight seconds, then it is likely to be a two-stop strategy. If instead the first refuelling stop runs to 10 or

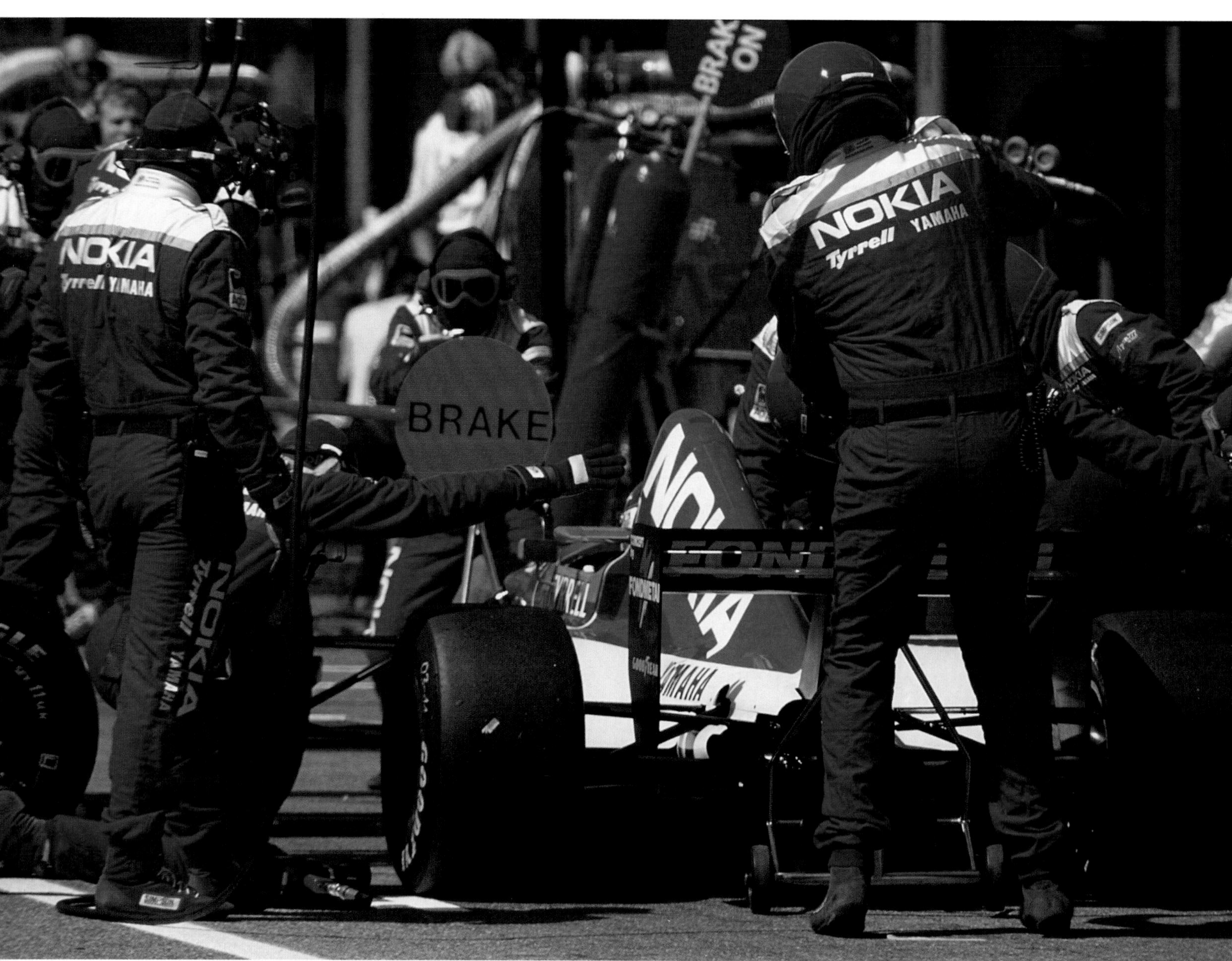

Pit and refueling stops have become a vital part of the planning of a race. In Tyrrell's case, it can be a way of overtaking faster cars, while for McLaren it can make the difference between a podium finish and humiliation.

11 seconds, then it is a one-stop strategy.

The rain is a problem in all of this, because if, for example, a car starts on wet weather tyres (deeply grooved), as the rain eases and the track dries, it will be looking to get on to slicks as early as possible. But if the team has decided on a one-stop strategy, this will lead to a re-appraisal of the race plan which could end up being disastrous. In Monaco, at the 1996 Grand Prix, the television commentators could not understand why so many drivers were not coming in for their tyre changes. The point was that they had to stay out, on the wrong tyres, so as to use up fuel, otherwise they would not be able to stick to their refuelling strategies.

The pit stop can also be used as a way of getting out of traffic. By coming in at the right time, and trying to second guess what the other teams are doing, it will allow some drivers to 'overtake' via the pit lane. This is something that was not on the agenda before refuelling came into Formula One this time round. Again, this is an advantage for the smaller teams which lack the power to overtake on the circuit.

Speed is of the essence during a pit stop and a crew can never practise enough.

Refuelling has also added a new dimension to the Sunday morning warm-up. Many of the teams indulge in a little poker. It goes like this. The cards are represented by the times posted in those morning laps. If a car goes faster than in qualifying, it would be pretty self-evident that it is carrying a light fuel load. As the Sunday warm-up is used to fine-tune the race set-up for each car, it would be logical to presume that cars posting unusually fast times in the warm-up would be going for a two- or three-stop strategy. Thus the other teams that would be battling for position with them, whether at the front of the grid, middle or even back, would tailor their race strategy accordingly. Poker is a game of skill, memory, and also bluff. And there is much bluffing going on the morning of a Grand Prix, with teams trying to outfox each other, looking for the narrowest of margins to take with them into the race.

Thus even more variables have been dialled into an already complicated sport. The Formula One engineering fraternity is often frustrated that much of the intricacy of motor racing is lost on the majority of the fans. The press, but even more so television, are looking for quick, easy answers, sound-bites that are easily digestible. So much is quite literally lost in translation.

For example, the role of the driver in the decision-making process to arrive at a team strategy is often overlooked. Senior racing drivers will be very pro-active in contributing to team tactics on race day. It is not unusual to change agreed strategy while on the grid. It may be that one of the engineers, who always have a discreet walk around the opposition's cars, gets on the team's headphones to warn of some set-up tweak which was not anticipated. Then the team manager will have a confab with the senior team members. When they have come to a conclusion, or a range of choices, they will then present them to the driver. Depending on the team, the decision may the driver's own, or the

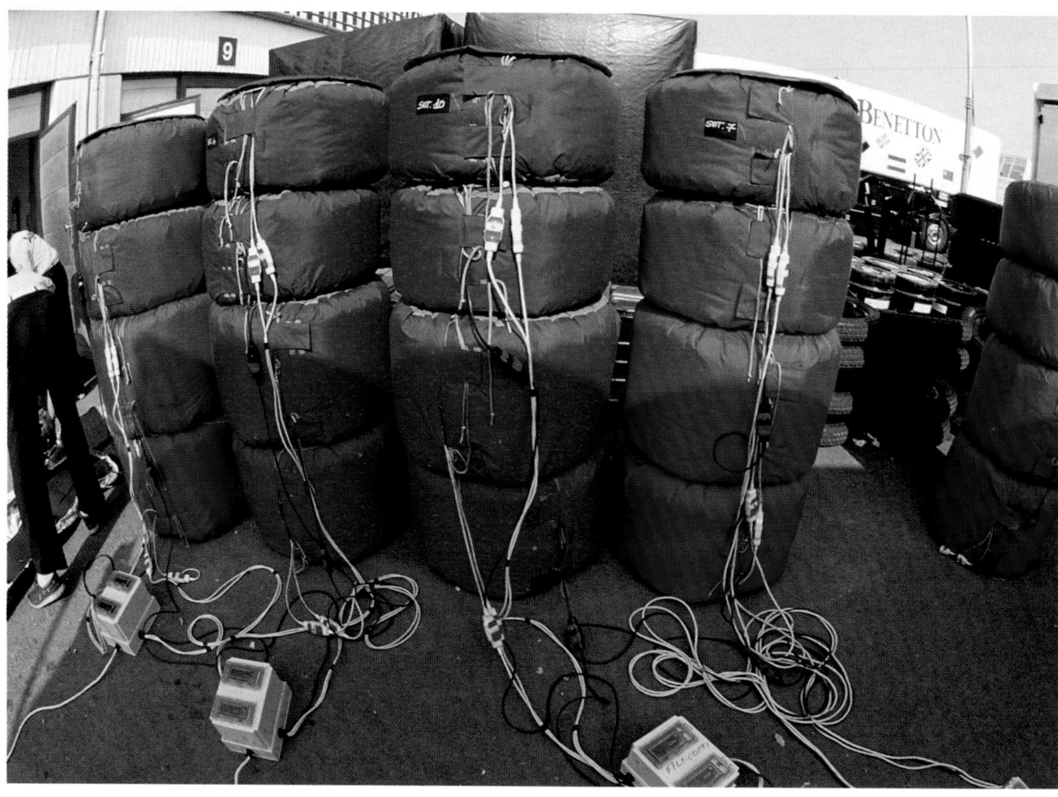

The limited number of tyres each team is allowed to use in a Grand Prix weekend makes for some interesting strategic decisions.

It was felt by many that had McLaren adopted a more decisive race strategy in Monaco, David Coulthard could have won the race.

Marlbo

team will try and steer him round to the decision they want him to take. The bottom line, though, is that no team wants drivers who are about to start a race feeling unhappy about the race strategy: they are likely to brood about it and not concentrate fully on the job of racing as fast as possible.

for the constructor. When Peugeot first entered Formula One, it supplied engines to McLaren. These engines, as one would expect in the early stages of development, had a habit of blowing up. The French press took great glee in publishing large pictures of McLaren cars with flames coming out of the

Mika Hakkinen and David Coulthard study telemetry printouts with their engineers and mechanics prior to the debrifing which will establish Sunday's race strategy.

engine. By the time the 1994 French Grand Prix came round, the McLaren staff were uncomfortably aware that about 20,000 Peugeot employees would be seated in the crowd at Magny-Cours, hoping to stuff their great national rivals, Renault. There was pressure, subtle and unspoken, on the team to run the cars in such a way that the risk of overheating would be minimized, so that the Peugeot big brass could save face. That meant not pushing 100 per cent, which is what Formula One cars are supposed to be doing at all times.

Taking decisions on the grid is not advisable. The structure of a Formula One team discourages thinking on one's feet. Every factor is methodically analyzed and logical conclusions are reached by the relevant people. Some teams operate more by committee, like McLaren, others, like Tyrrell, defer to one person who is solely in charge of strategy.

The bigger the team, the more pressure there is to change one's mind. The major engine manufacturers tend not to get involved in strategy meetings, until it is their own national race. Then the pressure mounts

Now that Mercedes partners McLaren, the pressure is doubled, as there are two races which take place in Germany. In 1995, in the rain, the team took completely the wrong decision regarding tyres, gambling that the rain was going to ease and the track would dry very quickly. With members of the Mercedes-Benz board in attendance in the pits, it was very painful for senior team members to see the Mercedes-McLarens disappear from the first page of the Tag-Heuer timing screens. This meant they had dropped so far back on the track that they were vying for position with the Minardis and the Fortis. The pressure of having, for the first time, so many senior representatives from the engine partner, got the better of the usually well-oiled McLaren decision-making machine. Officially it was the drivers who took the decision. In reality they too felt the pressure. The resulting 'committee camel' was the unfortunate result.

Some of the senior team members who spend the race on the pit wall, adapting, or not, the strategies they worked out and agreed on earlier, are in no doubt that this aspect of motor racing will become ever more important. The difficulty for the public is that it is very hard to capture the excitement of it from the television images or the newspaper reports. Nevertheless, this is where many of the races are going to be won and lost in the years to come and where drivers, in part sidelined from other areas of the decision-making process, will be able to make a significant contribution.

CEA
EAGLE

Safety

The death of Ayrton Senna and the subsequent spate of accidents in 1994 prompted a review of all aspects of safety at Formula One races.

It was felt by many that the tragic Grand Prix at Imola in 1994, when Roland Ratzenberger and Ayrton Senna died, was the watershed in all matters regarding safety in Formula One racing. But it would be misleading to think that the issue of driver and circuit safety was not taken seriously by the sport's governing body, the FIA, or indeed FOCA, the Formula One Constructor's Association.

Yet, subconsciously, the sport had become relatively complacent after so many years of tragedy-free racing. The hunched figure of Martin Donnelly on the circuit at Estoril served as a reminder that serious injury was never far away. But since that accident, further improvements had been made to the chassis and to the car.

But such was the deep-seated popular, and governmental, reaction to the tragic deaths at Imola, and to the freakish sequence of accidents which happened to Rubens Barrichello, Karl Wendlinger and Andrea Montermini in the same period that year, that the sport's authorities were impelled to establish new lines of thinking on the complicated and emotional issue of safety. Suddenly, beneath the glitz of the sponsors' branding, the glamour of the paddock girls, the excesses of the corporate fat cats, motor racing was dangerous once more.

In some ways, though, it is the drivers themselves who have been the most half-hearted about their own safety. For them it is a mixture of wanting to do what they have longed to do since they were children, of a feeling that they owe to sponsors and team owners, and also that their natural macho nature – 'it can't happen to me' – precludes them from complaining about adverse racing conditions, be they meteorological, to do with track design or car safety. Many of the media who have been covering Formula One for a while know that some of the smaller teams will cut corners: it's the drivers themselves who'll admit it. Yet they are still willing to drive, battling at the back of the grid, for the chance of one day being spotted by one of the big teams. It rarely happens.

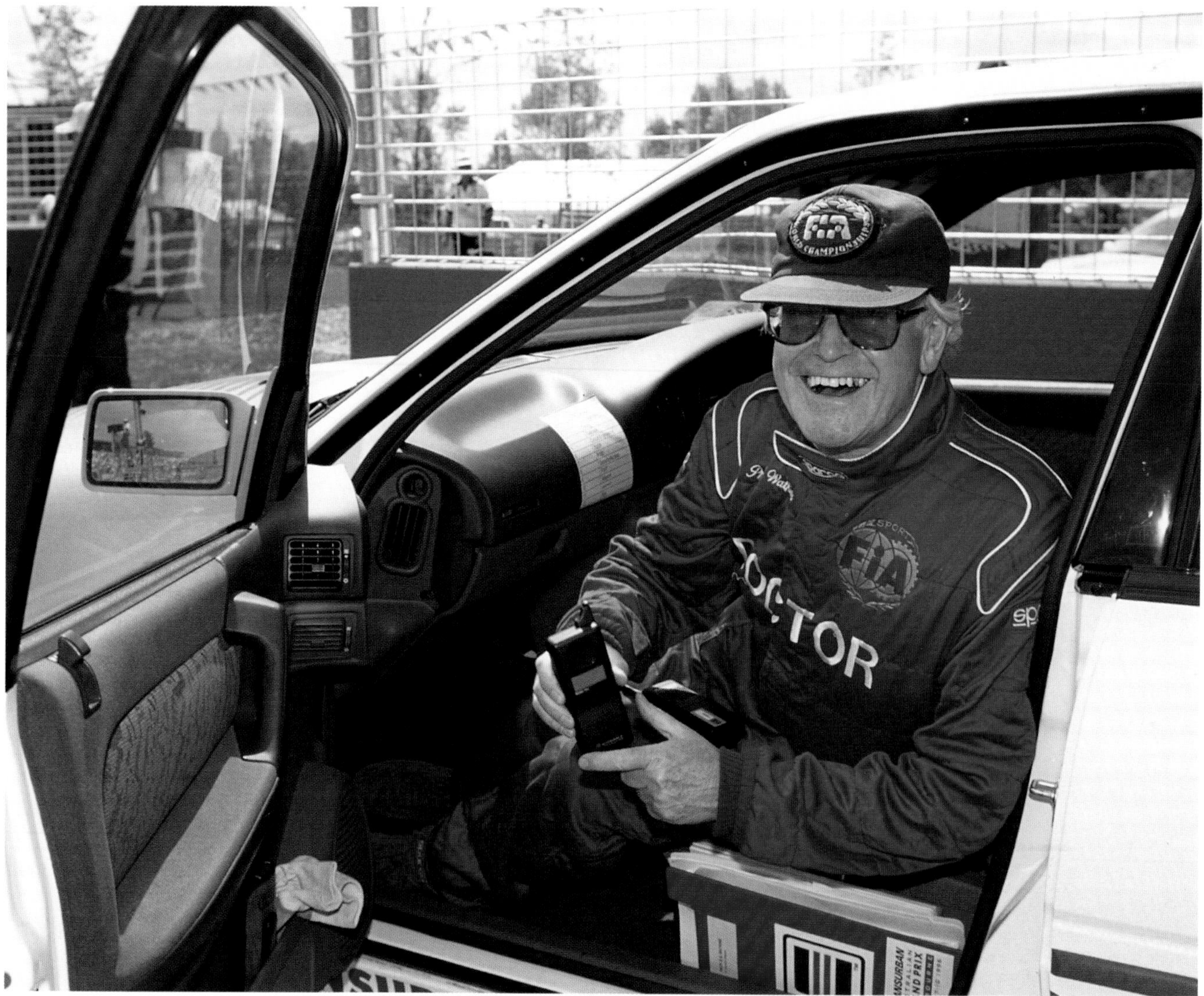

As with so many things in Formula One, it was Bernie Ecclestone, the president of FOCA, who made the first significant move. It was 1978, the year that Ronnie Peterson died in an Italian hospital of complications arising out from an operation on his legs. Ecclestone asked professor Sid Watkins, a London-based neuro-surgeon, to take charge of medical care at the Grands Prix. Professor Watkins had already been involved in organizing the medical backup at races in the United States and in Great Britain. It was clear that the sport needed a unified approach to medical care: some countries were significantly better than others at dealing with the injuries that could occur in Formula One. The lack of a coherent approach meant that the standards of care could vary greatly.

Professor Watkin's medical commission set stringent standards for trackside safety. All circuits had to conform, with a set number of doctors and paramedics stationed along the race track, a fully equipped accident and emergency unit on site – with surgeons and re-animation specialists – ambulances, medical cars and helicopters. Professor Watkins is always present, sitting alongside a race driver in a fast saloon car, linked by radio.When there is an accident, he is driven at high speed to the scene of the crash. In normal circumstances, the first officials who arrive will wait for the 'Prof', as he is affectionately called by all in Formula One. Under his supervision, the driver will be dealt with following a set of standard, and well-rehearsed, procedures.

The chief medical officer for each Grand Prix has to fill in a questionnaire and submit it to the FIA two months before a race. Numbers and focus can vary greatly from circuit to circuit. At Monaco there are 100 doctors stationed around the principality's street circuit, backed up by three intervention cars. In Spain there are no doctors, but there are ten intervention cars. In Hungary there is a doctor at each corner, backed up by an ambu-

lance and there are three intervention cars

The immediate aftermath of an accident is often the most crucial time. When Mika Hakkinen crashed in Adelaide in 1995, he had expert medical attention within 30 seconds of his McLaren hitting the barriers. The doctor on duty at that particular spot was a re-animation specialist. Professor Watkins was there within three minutes. There is no doubt that the Finnish driver owes his life to this speedy reaction, which is a direct consequence of the work done by the FIA's medical commission, setting very high standards in all of the Grand Prix circuits.

Professor Watkins is also closely involved with nominated hospitals in the vicinity of the circuits. These too are inspected and have to conform to stringent standards.

Yet all in Formula One, particularly the medical staff, would prefer that drivers do not get injured in the first place. This is where the time after the 1994 San Marino Grand Prix became such an important mark for the further development of safety in motor racing. Now that the medical side was as good as it could be in the circumstances, steps had to be taken to improve the cars and the circuits.

Much work was already happening on the cars, and McLaren was already leading the way with its own research in special impact-absorbing foam, feasibility studies with air-bag technology and the development of side-impact materials to be built within the advanced composite fibre chassis, the safety cell, which had already saved so many drivers from major injuries. Other teams were also carrying out their own research in these areas.

In order to streamline these efforts and once more bring a unified response to issues that were bound to cause a certain degree of controversy – not least the matter that safety-inspired design changes always cost money to the teams – the FIA turned once more to Professor Watkins, appointing him as chairman of the newly formed Experts Advisory Group. This had wide-ranging powers and it was detailed to advise the FIA's Technical Working Group – made up by a number of senior engineers from different teams – which is the only authority in the sport with the power to change the technical regulations.

Under the chairmanship of Professor Watkins, and with the considerable financial backing of the FIA – said to be in the region of £500,000 – the advisory group has concentrated on a number of issues. These can be broadly divided between active and pas-

The immediate aftermath of an accident is often the most crucial time. When Mika Hakkinen crashed in 1995 he had expert medical attention within 30 seconds of hitting the barriers.

sive safety. The former is usually linked to the racing cars and the drivers, while the latter has to do with circuits.

The changes to the circuit layout have been the most high profile, at least in media terms. The controversy surrounding the felling of trees at Monza, the changes at Spa-Francorchamps and at Silverstone were widely discussed in the world's press. There was much talk of circuits being emasculated, of Formula One becoming boring and of drivers not liking the new design of some of the circuits. The reality was that it was the drivers themselves, under the guise of the Grand Prix Drivers' Association, who recommended a number of these circuit alterations.

Professor Watkins brought in scientific analysis where before there was just intuition and experience. 'We are investigating the trajectory a car will take, under different circumstances, as it exits a bend. On the basis of this we site the gravel traps, we look at the co-efficient of friction, we study the depth of the gravel,' says the neuro-surgeon. With the deadpan humour which has long been his trademark, he also adds that 'there's a lot of gravel in the world, and it's all different'. This kind of problem, and the relish with which the 'Prof' sets about solving it, is the reason why Max Mosley, the FIA president, appointed him in the first place, or as the Prof would have it. 'Max let me loose on this. But he must take lots of the credit. His was a low-key, considered and responsible response.'

Equally important, if of lower profile, was the work undertaken at MIRA, a goverment-sponsored agency which specializes in research for the motor industry. Here, for months on end, Formula One chassis are subjected to intense G-forces. The area of the cockpit has in particular come under scrutiny. Karl Wendlinger's injuries would have been avoided, or at least greatly diminished by the high-sided design which is obligatory nowadays. In Montreal this year, both Gerhard Berger and Jean Alesi crashed in a way that would have led to both drivers being injured had the high-sided Benetton

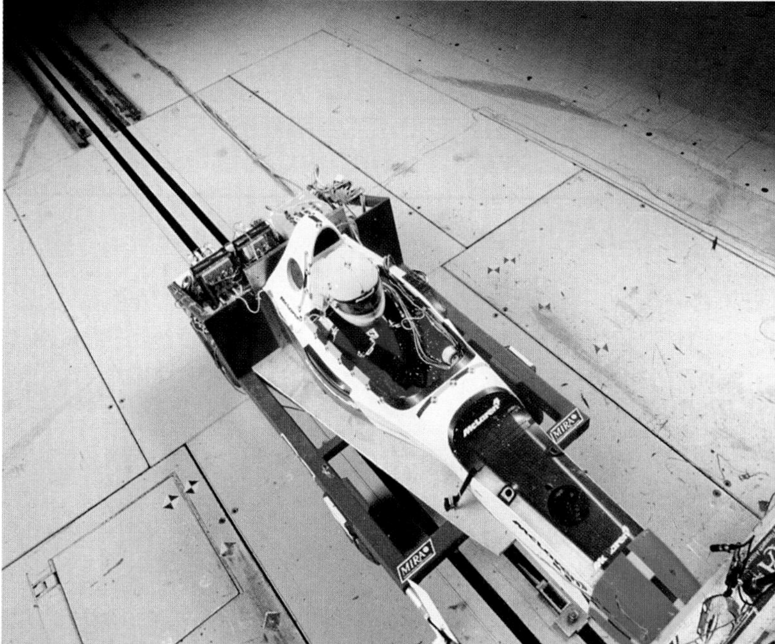

cockpit not protected them. Flavio Briatore, not a man who thanks many people, made it his business to thank Charley Whiting, the FIA's technical delegate, whose job it is to make sure that the safety recommendations are implemented by the teams.

Now the research is focused on air bags, but there are a number of difficulties to be overcome. One of them has to do with the trigger point at which a bag will be released: a 3G sudden deceleration in a race is not uncommon. There is also research into the shape of the air bag: it is known that if a passenger raises his or her hands to protect the face (a common enough reaction) this could lead to broken wrists.

But the most far-reaching project is one that will see all teams fitting an 'accident data recorder' to the cockpit in 1997. This electronic gadget will sense and log a wide variety of data arising from the car's behaviour, up to and including an accident. Its 12 channels will be powered by the car's electrics, but will also have its own power supply to last it nearly a minute after the car has crashed.

The £6,000 device will be fitted on a Thursday and returned to the FIA on a Sunday. It is meant to be tamper-proof and will be placed underneath the fuel tank at the back of the car. The FIA is confident this device will help hugely in the analysis of accidents and also in the understanding of the areas of the car that need improving from the point of view of safety.

'The teams have been great,' said Professor Watkins. 'They do squawk every now and then about the cost, but they soon come round and accept our thinking.' He doesn't say it, of course, but the reality is that a fit driver is a lot more use than an injured one. And the sponsors would heartily go along with that. Theirs is an investment, after all.

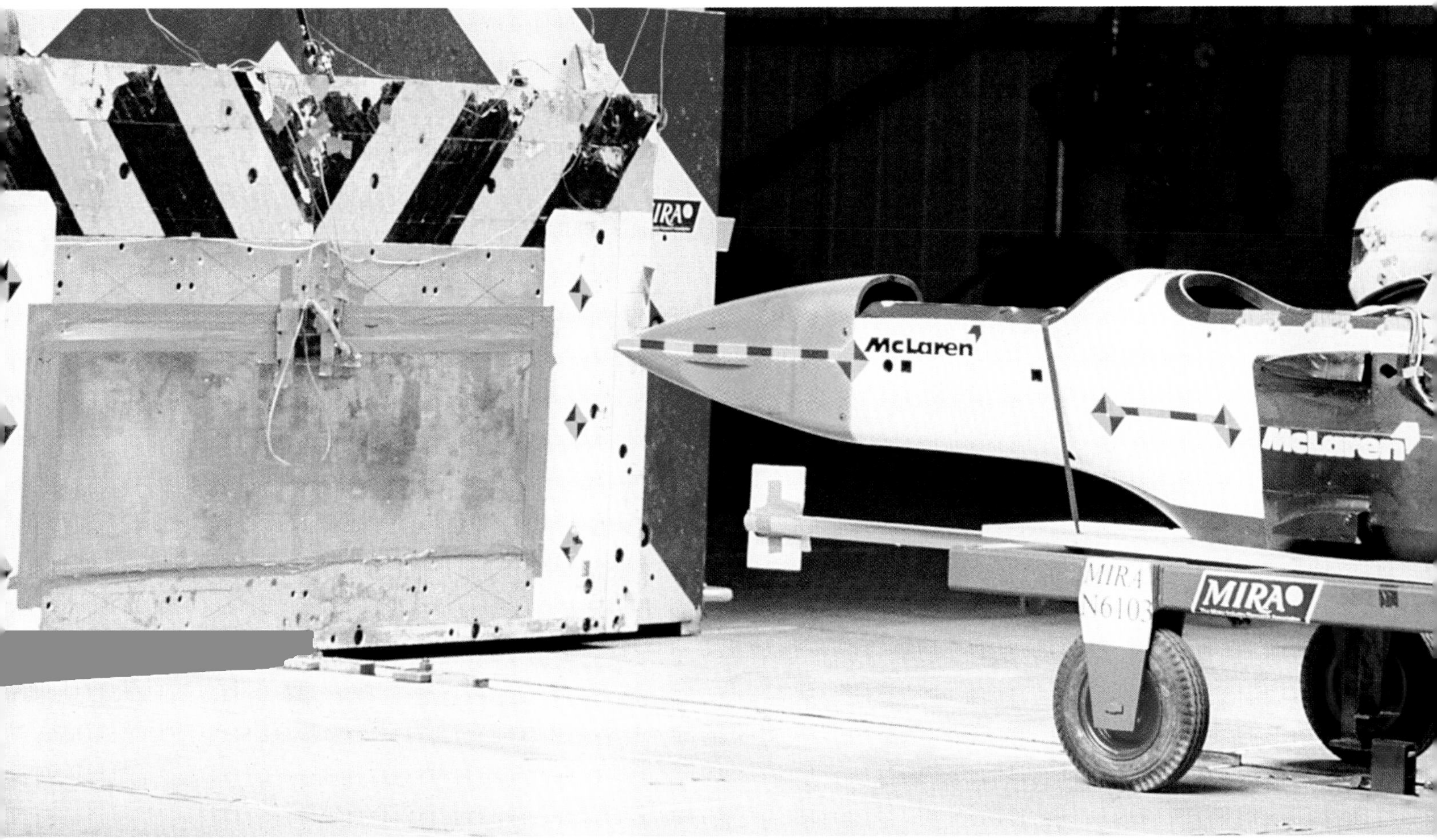
MIRA
McLaren
McLaren
MIRA
N6103
MIRA

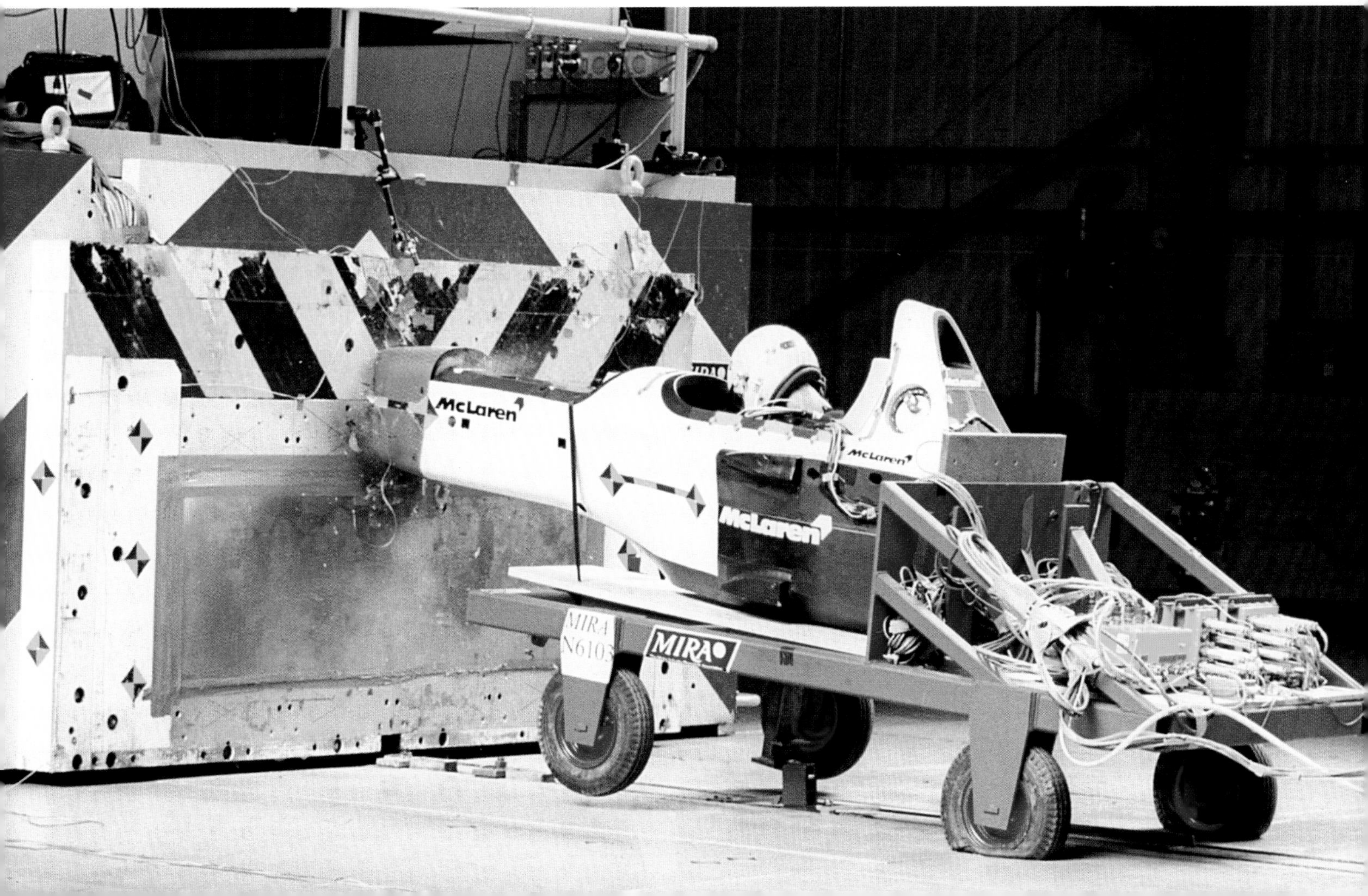
McLaren
McLaren
McLaren
MIRA
N6103
MIRA

I will never forget the immediate aftermath of the fire in the Benetton pits, when Jos Verstappen's car caught fire after a fuel nozzle leaked during his stop. I, as many McLaren team members not directly involved in the nitty-gritty of race day operations, had cleared out of the pits after the race start.

Like many others, we watched the race cocooned in the air-conditioned unreality of the motor homes, listening to 'Watty' (John Watson) on the Eurosport channel. That's where we saw it first, the ball of flame engulfing the Benetton pit crew and the driver. It took what seemed ages to realize that this was 'here', at the circuit, not 'there' on the television screens, and that our pits were next door to the ones where the fire was. People screamed inside the motor homes. I rushed out, not knowing whether I should go anywhere near the pits at all. I was not wearing flame-proof overalls, I am not trained in first aid. In short, I would not have a clue what to do if confronted by flames and injured people. Nevertheless I ran on, thinking that I would have some sort of function as the person in charge of media for my team. Clearly, whatever the damage, there would be much to talk about afterwards and McLaren, as one of the big teams which had already voiced unofficial opposition to refueling, would be asked its opinion.

Entering from the back door in our garage, I was confronted by the sight of our guys looking as they had never before. There is a cliché about smelling fear: there certainly was a very weird smell to our garage, stronger than that of fire extinguishers and sweat. It was animal, and many of the mechanics looked as if they had stepped over that boundary between human and animal, when adrenalin takes over from the rational mind. Their eyes were bulging, many had ripped off their overalls, some had scorch marks on them. There was mostly

Pit Stops

silence, except for one of the mechanics who was zeroing in on a photographer calling him all the names under the sun. Feeling totally inadequate – what do you say to people who have had their worst nightmare happen? – I seized on this confrontation about to happen as a way of doing something useful. I ushered the photographer out of the garage.

When I went back in later on, I found out that some of our boys had run to help the Benetton mechanics, that some had jumped on the burning Benetton people and smothered the flames with their own bodies covered in flame-proof overalls and that others had run back into the pits screaming for water, where there was none to be found. All were shaken, the usual toungue-in-cheek

Each team has in its garage an exotic cocktail of highly combustible fuels.

(Opposite)Formula One mechanics must protect themselves from the very real dangers presented by modern day refueling.

BRAKES
ON

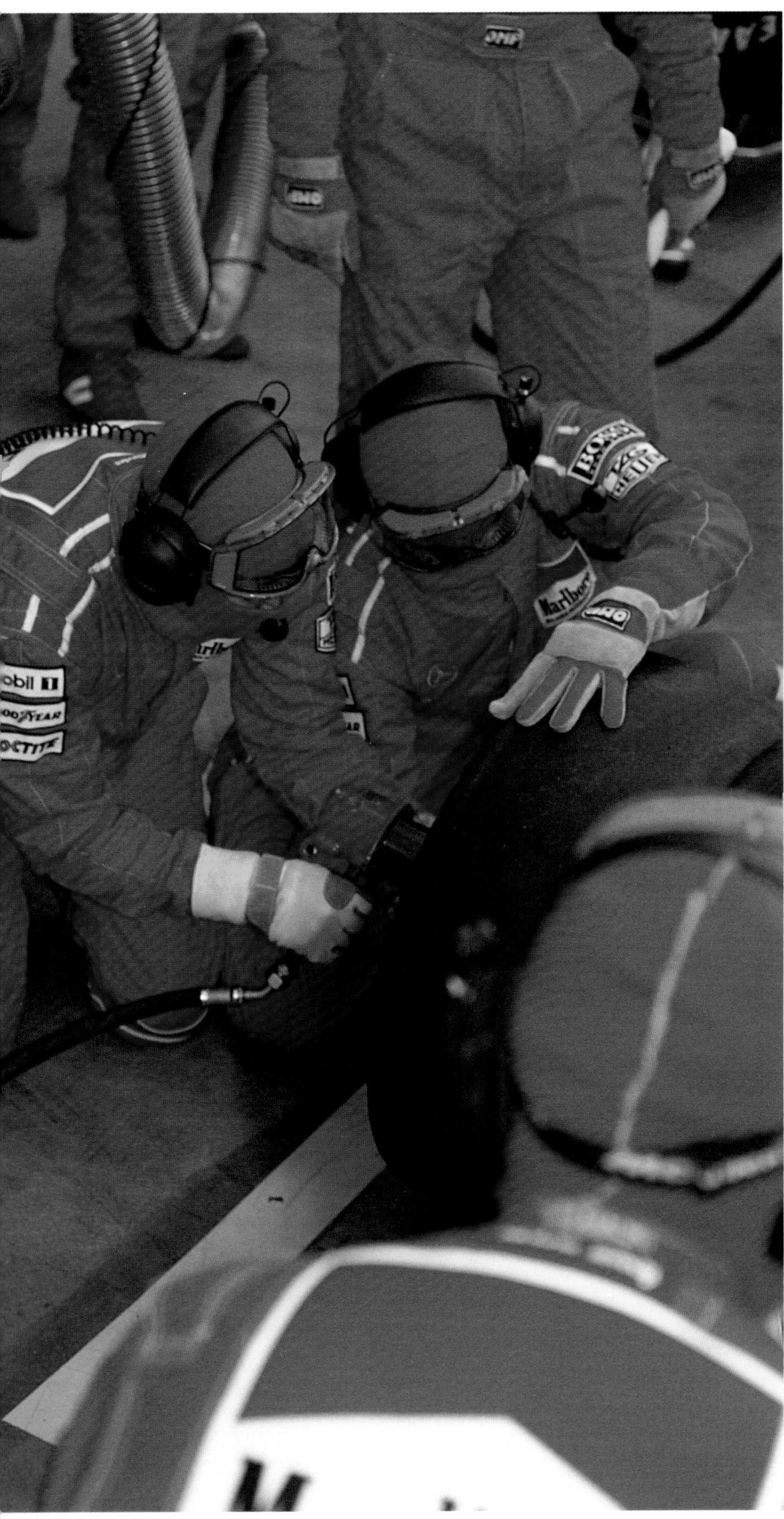

macho posing so common to all pit crews was deeply irrelevant. Death had had a wander round the pits and no one liked it one bit.

In the days that followed, Formula One once more came under the scrutiny of the media, of health and safety bodies. Photographs were published showing that the flames had leapt as high as the hospitality units above the pits and that had the wind caught the flames, the chief executives of some of the biggest blue-chip companies in the world would have, quite simply, fried.

The sport's authorities tried to minimize the damage, the fuel rigs were re-inspected, ridiculous rumours circulated that maybe the Benetton fuel-hose mechanics were not quite strong enough to hold it in place, and so on.

In the end, refuelling survived the onslaught. Other drivers had accidents in the pit lane, meanwhile the fuel rigs kept being improved, although many of the older mechanics in a number of teams have called it a day and have made way for younger pit crews who accept more readily the inherent dangers of refuelling. By their own admission, the teams do not take into account the element of danger when deciding on the number of pit stops a team will have in a race.

In fact, the pit crews themselves are quite supportive of the whole process. They have always been proud of the speed with which four tyres could be changed. It is an area where the mechanics feel their role is crucial – which it is – and there is a feeling among them that this is real racing. This is not the mumbo-jumbo of electronics, this is hands-on, tangible and can make the difference to the outcome of the Grand Prix. This is still racing at its purest.

There is more to a pit stop than meets the eye, quite literally. It all starts back in the factory at the close of season, when the team manager and the chief mechanic start the selection process for the refuelling and tyre-change crew. Some mechanics will have left, others will not want to travel to the races any more. Thus the team manager sifts through the options and, like a football manager, will try to assemble a balanced team to last the season and one which will develop a strong sense of pride in their job.

Once the team is chosen, the priority shifts to kitting it out properly. In the early days of re-fuelling, most teams went their own way, but after observing each other, most now use the same, or very similiar equipment. Particular attention is devoted to

(previous pages) Pit lane fires have become an occupational hazard for all Formula One mechanics.

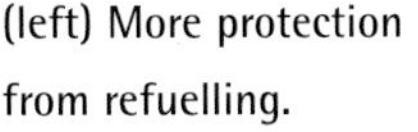

(left) More protection from refuelling.

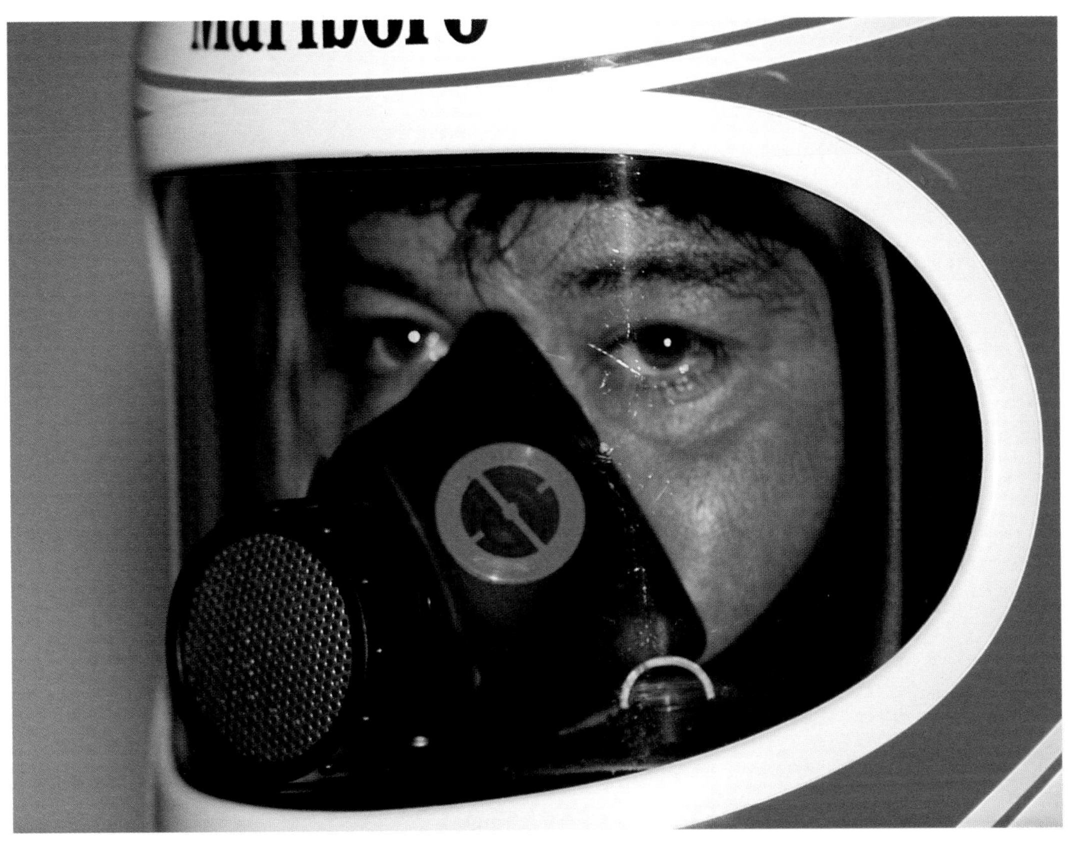

(opposite) A pit lane crew can change four tyres on a car in less than five seconds.

There is more to a pit stop than meets the eye. When the 20 people descend on the car, they will always change four tyres, refuel, clear the radiators and clean the driver's visor.

the two men who have to hold the fuel hose and who usually wear breathing apparatus. The team is now ready, mentally and physically for the pit stops.

seconds.

All of this does not come easy. There is much practising, usually when all the media and the sponsors, the people the mechanics

Despite the dangers, those assigned to the pit stops are immensely proud to be part of such an elite team within the team.

When the 20 people converge on the car with military precision, they will always change four tyres, refuel, clear the radiators and clean the driver's visor. In addition they might also change the wing settings, open the auxiliary oil tank and check the brake cooling. All of this in about seven seconds. Then, if required, a nose cone can be changed in 20 consider to be Formula One 'groupies', are long gone from the circuit, or have not risen from their beds. This is when the car is wheeled in, time and time again, to the right position, where the front and rear jack men go to work, lifting the 550-kilo race car and driver off the ground. There are three men at each wheel, in goes the air gun, off comes the wheel, on comes the next, on goes the air gun. Meanwhile, the fuel nozzle has been positioned and pushed into its slot. These two mechanics are usually air-tight, with their own independent breathing apparatus. Behind them others are checking the fuel rig. Standing by are men with fire extinguishers, others are checking the car, one is supporting it from the opposite side of the fuel nozzle. The car is earthed and the data is being sent to the telemetry positions inside the pits.

It is an incredible sight. The car comes in alone, the 'lollipop man' waves it in. It is swarmed over. Then it's alone again, going down the pit lane on to the circuit to fight another battle. The chief mechanic will say a laconic, but heartfelt, 'well done lads, thank you' to the crew through their headphones. The pit stop is a tense and exhausting few seconds for all involved, but while the race continues, there is little time for relaxation, only preparation for and concentration on the next time.

The mechanics are very proud of being part of the pit crew. They will often ask photographers for pictures. For many of them, Formula One means being part of the best, slickest, fastest pit crew in the pit lane. It's all about team spirit, and the mechanics are the ones who keep it alive and relevant in a sport that too often forgets that bloody-mindedness and passion is what the fans want out of motor racing.

Drivers are an integral part of the pit stop – they must keep the engine revving, apply the brakes and ensure they don't stall or exceed the speed limit as they roar out of the pit lane.

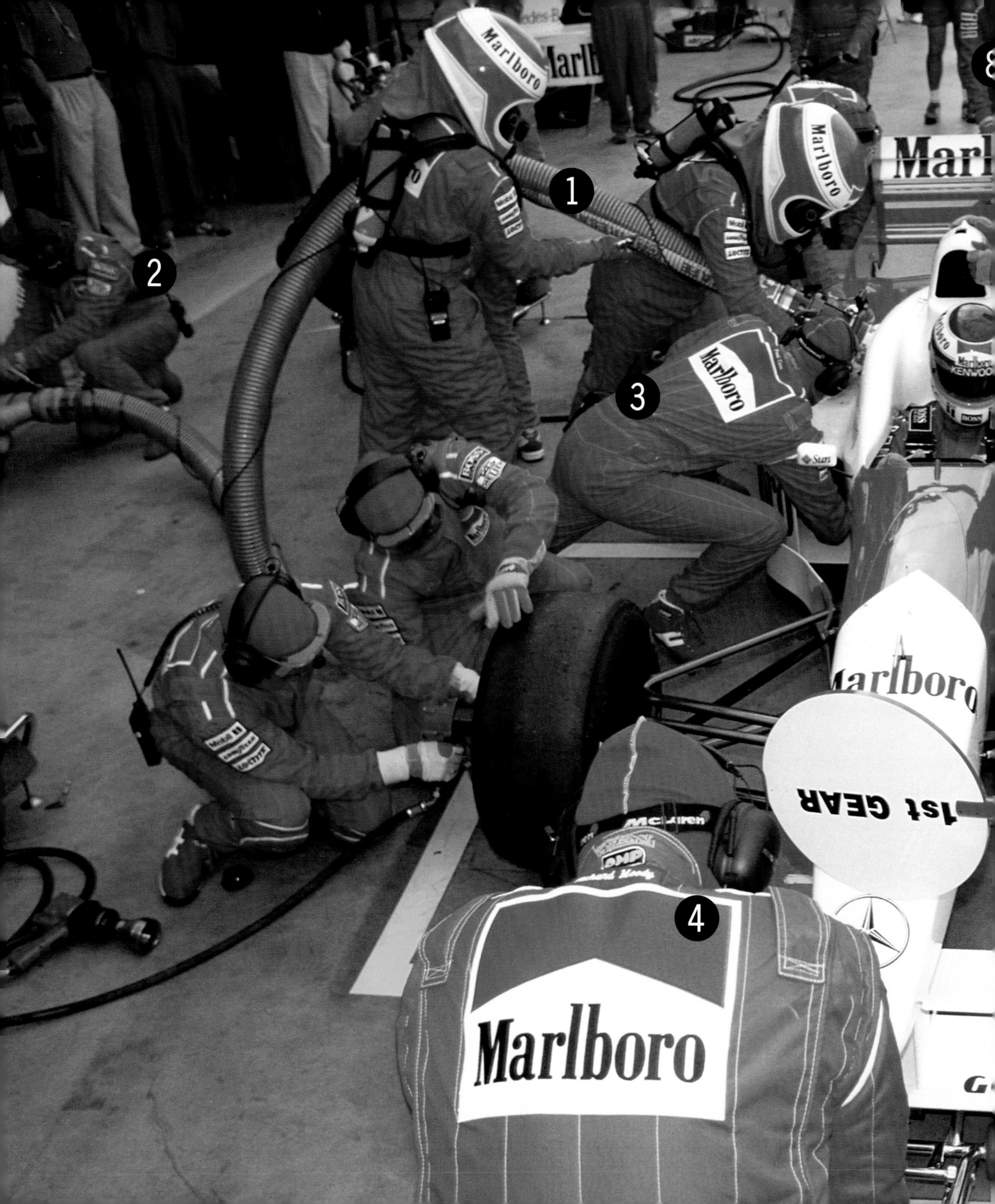

Marlboro
1
2
3
4
Marlboro
McLaren
KENWOOD
Marlboro

① TWO MEN TO REFUEL
Both volunteers – they breath compressed air.

② EXTRA FUEL MAN
Usually engineer in charge of refuelling rig.

③ SPARE MAN
Usually clears out radiator ducts, cleans driver's visor etc.

④ FRONT JACK MAN
Car stops inches from his legs – uses hydraulic jack.

⑤ 'LOLLY POP MAN'
Usually chief mechanic – He is in charge of pit stop.

⑥ 3 MEN PER TYRE
One takes old wheel off, second man puts new one in place, third has air gun.

⑦ SPARE MAN
Holds car steady when jacked up and being refuelled.

⑧ REAR JACK MAN
Uses manual jack, so has to be strong.

Australia / Brazil / Argentina

The inaugural race of the seaon was held in Melbourne, the first time the city has hosted a Formula One race.

The 1996 season started with three overseas races. The first, in Melbourne, was especially important for Marlboro McLaren Mercedes: added to the unknown quantity of a new circuit, the team had a new car, a new driver in David Coulthard and, in Mika Hakkinen, a driver who was still recovering from a life-threatening accident he had in Adelaide in the last race of the 1995 season. There was also Alain Prost, brought in to be part of the Technical Working Group, a sort of steering committee within McLaren which pools together expertise from the whole company.

The completion of the three new cars had been delayed by a number of hitches back at Woking and many spares had been flown out at the last moment, enabling the mechanics to finish building them on Wednesday night.

Despite these unknown factors, the mood in the team was upbeat. The testing at Silverstone and Estoril had gone well and everyone was eager to get stuck in and contest races for the first time since Ayrton Senna's win in Adelaide in 1993, the last time McLaren had won a race.

But qualifying in Melbourne revealed an all-too-familiar problem with McLaren: the car was hard to set up and struggling with a lack of grip. From being the fastest in winter testing, it was now 1.6 seconds slower than Formula One newcomer Jacques Villeneuve's

Races

... All the hard work over the winter seemed to have come to nothing and there was a feeling that it would be more of the same for a while longer.

Williams, which was on pole. And that was with Mika Hakkinen in the driving seat. As for David Coulthard, a race winner the previous season, he was languishing in 13th place. The engine, though an improvement on last year's, still showed a lack of power in the low revs, as well as 'holes' in the power band. Thus it had plenty of power, but it was not delivered smoothly, which made the car hard to drive and unpredictable. In the race Hakkinen drove steadily and finished in fifth place. Coulthard had to retire, due to throttle problems, on lap 24 after switching to the spare car following his involvement in Martin Brundle's accident at the end of the starting straight. The team was very down after these results: all the hard work over the winter, the late nights, the long test sessions seemed to have come to nothing and there was a feeling that it would be more of the same for a while longer.

Two weeks later in Brazil the pattern repeated itself. Hakkinen qualified in seventh place, Coulthard in 14th, more than three seconds adrift from Hill's pole position. The Finn once more drove sensibly, and after a long battle with his fellow countryman Mika Salo in a Tyrrell, finished a creditable fourth. His Scottish team mate had another rough day at the races. During the morning warm-up his Mercedes engine failed after only a couple of laps. He had a very good race start and overtook five cars in the first lap. But he spun off track when he was in seventh place and had to do it all over again from 14th. He came in for tyres on lap 22 and came out again wearing slicks. The rain started once more and he went off once again on lap 29,

(following pages) Luca Badoer has an uncomfortable moment at the Argentine Grand Prix.

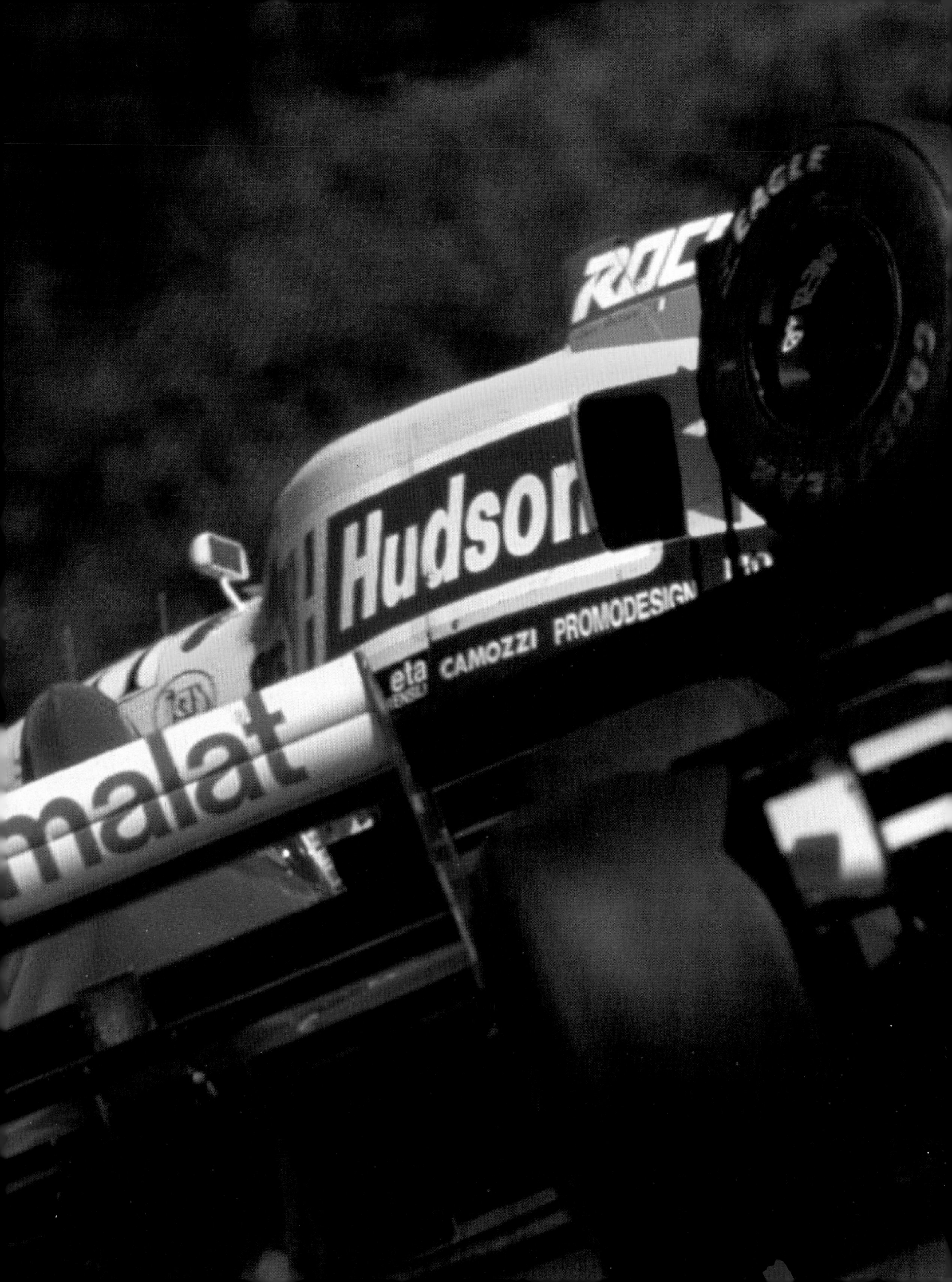
PROMODESIGN
CAMOZZI
eta

ORTI
22

this time for good.

Some people in the team were beginning to get a little worried about the new arrival from Williams. He was clearly finding it hard to adapt to a very nervous car. He and his race engineer, David Brown, who had also come from Williams lured by a six-figure salary, were finding the going tough. But that was understandable, others would say. The Williams was a great car and ours was, well, not so good. Driver and engineer needed time to settle down. Yet it was clear that Coulthard seemed ill at ease with a nervous car. In some instances he'd back off. But Hakkinen could handle this sort of car better. Maybe he'd had a little more practice: this was his third year at McLaren as a full-time driver, and before that he'd been the test driver. Whatever the reason, it was felt that Coulthard may not be the kind of driver McLaren had hoped he would be. Mika had acquitted himself well, yet he too was coming under intense scrutiny in the pits. His habit of hiding behind dark glasses – a shyness about one of his eyes, still a little lazy after his accident – and a new-found brusqueness of manner, did not endear him to some of the more seasoned members of the team. They felt they could – just – take that kind of behaviour from world champions, but this was not one of them.

After two races it was a struggle to keep morale high. Though Hakkinen had done reasonably well, the team was not where it would have liked to have been in terms of competitiveness. A fourth and a fifth place is really not good enough for McLaren whose mission statement includes the words 'to win every Formula One race'. No one at Woking has forgotten the words said by Dennis in

The magnificent sight of a Formula One grid assembled for the fray at the beginning of a race.

The narrow pit lane in Monaco is an anachronism in modern day grand Prix racing.

Monaco in 1994 when he greeted Martin Brundle's second place with the comment that 'coming second is the first of the losers'. Added to this was a car that was described by the one driver who seemed to know how to handle it as lacking in front-end grip. This meant that as the car went into a corner, the driver did not know whether it would turn or go straight. This was the problem Nigel Mansell complained about the year before. On top of this, the engine was not delivering the power smoothly. This meant that it might be slow coming out of a corner and then, when the revs climbed, it could suddenly delivered a kick leaving the driver to fight a rear end which is trying to step out. In short, no front-end grip coming into corners, no rear-end grip coming out. Not surprisingly the young Scottish driver was struggling.

Some of the more energetic team members managed to get some R & R in Brazil before going to Buenos Aires for the Argentine Grand Prix. Once more, this was to become a character-forming experience. Despite much promise in the early part of the weekend, qualifying was a frustrating affair and Hakkinen lined up for the start in eighth place, just 0.2 of a second in front of a more settled Coulthard in ninth place. The Scotsman had another great getaway from the middle of the pack and was fifth at the end of the first lap. But there the lack of competitiveness of the McLaren-Mercedes was cruelly exposed as it became apparent that Coulthard was losing a second per lap to the cars in front of him. Hakkinen lasted only 19 laps, sidelined by a throttle failure. His team mate got to as high as a fourth, eventually finishing just out of the points in seventh place.

The tough three-race overseas spell was now over, and Formula One was going back to its spiritual home in Europe. But amidst all the noise about Williams, Hill, Villeneuve and Schumacher, some of the more experienced voices in the sport, both in the media and within the paddock, were expressing surprise at the lack of competitiveness of McLaren. One commentator reminded his readers of one of Dennis' least fortunate remarks to the media – 'We make history, you just write about it' – and opined that that kind of attitude was at the root of the sniggering that went on within the motor homes every time a red-and-white car had to retire.

Wet weather racing is one of the most dramatic aspects of the Formula One spectacle.

European/San Marino/Monaco

After three disappointing races, McLaren reacted in typically robust style and a major redesign of the car was ordered. The new car was meant to race in Monaco, but a lack of spares pushed its debut back to the Spanish Grand Prix. In order to fix the handling problems, the McLaren designers decided to build a shorter car, which would also suit the many races where tight and twisty circuits were preferred to long-flowing ones.

The effort of designing and building a new car, even though many of the components remained the same, was the sort of thing that McLaren could achieve: its huge resources of manpower and finance ensured this. But many in the pit lane wondered why, for the second year running, did McLaren have to have a second bite at making a competitive car? Granted that cars are never 'born' perfect, but this was not a question of fine-tuning, but of a rebuild.

Meanwhile, Coulthard was beginning to get the measure of the car. The Scotsman was third in the European Grand Prix at the Nurburgring, led the race for 16 laps in Imola and finished second in Monaco in the revised model. Such was his change of fortunes that Britain's Autosport magazine dedicated its cover to him on the eve of the Spanish Grand Prix. 'McLaren's Mr Motivator' and 'The next step is victory, says David Coulthard'. Autosport also made much of Coulthard's brilliant starts in four out of the six races he had so far competed in. As is so often the case, the magazine unwittingly cast a voodoo spell on him: the McLaren driver had his worst ever race in Spain, crashing into the back of another car in the rain after qualifying in 14th place. Hakkinen, who had to retire in Germany, was eighth in Imola and in Monaco, fared a little better in Spain finishing in fifth place, though team pride was not salvaged by the two points as the Finn had been lapped. This is not something that goes down very well at McLaren.

Despite the intense rivalry, there is also heartfelt camaraderie amongst the drivers.

One of the questions which arise with certain regularity is how long will the board of Mercedes-Benz suffer the indignity of being also-rans in Formula One. At the European Grand Prix, Dennis and Norbert Haug, the head of the Motorsport division of the German car manufacturer, met with the board, sparking off all sorts of speculative stories. In reality this was a regular meeting where the Mercedes brass is updated on the progress of the team. There is no doubt that Haug is under pressure to deliver, and the effort that Mercedes put into this task is a big one. Nevertheless, blown engines in qualifying are of no help to his

The agony and the ecstasy: Sometimes a fraction of a second makes the difference between a podium place or (opposite) an excursion into the 'cat litter'.

cause within Mercedes-Benz. By the end of the weekend though, German smiles were less tense: Coulthard was on the podium and the new spec engine had proved its worth.

A feature of the Spanish race was the amount of hand luggage McLaren personnel carried with them throughout the weekend. Spares for the new car were being made, immediately packed and handed over to whoever was next on his or her way to Heathrow. The new car had also posted some very good times in testing at Silverstone, so the disappointment was once more palpable in the McLaren pits. So much effort, so little reward. What Dennis had described as a 'lack of competitiveness in races' was still not being resolved.

Canada/France/GB/Germany/Hungary

Mika Hakkinen finished fifth in the Canadian Grand Prix after qualifying in sixth place, his best showing since the start of the season. Again lack of grip was what the Finn blamed for his inability to get up higher on the grid. Hakkinen also tested a new electronic brake balance system, which moves the braking focus to the front brakes as the driver squeezes the pedal harder. But the system was not entirely satisfactory and it was sidelined for more testing. David Coulthard qualified further back, in 10th place, the victim of an interrupted session after an accident involving Gerhard Berger's Benetton. The Scot had an uncharacteristic bad start, then took advantage of a few retirements ahead of him and together with his team mate moved up ahead of the Jordans thanks to better pit stops. Coulthard finished fourth, 17 seconds ahead of his team mate. The race was won by Damon Hill, who opted for two-stop strategy and though he rejoined behind Jacques Villeneuve, who was on one, he showed how much he has improved as a driver by reeling in the Canadian and stopping him from a fairy-tale win on the circuit named after his father Gilles.

The news in France was that the Williams-Renault were quite perfect. Damon Hill won the French Grand Prix, while the Ferraris were lurching from bad to worse,

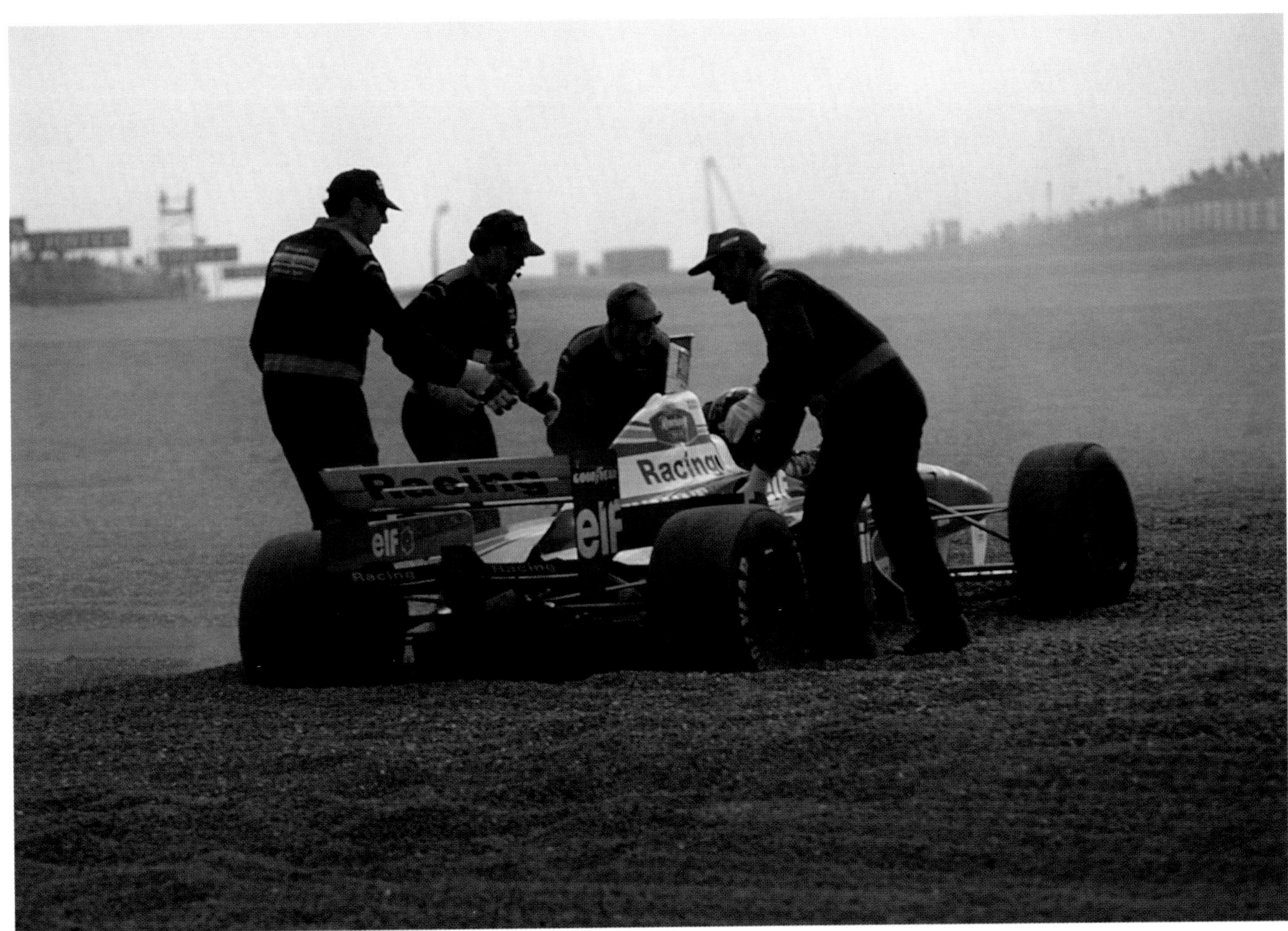

The crowds love to see their heroes, regardless of the car they may be in.

with the extraordinary sight of Michael Schumacher, world champion, unable to even start the race. The McLaren drivers kept up the momentum they showed in Canada by finishing in the points, Mika Hakkinen in use the shorter car, though it was originally intended for the more twisty circuits. It suited Hakkinen's driving style and he showed well in qualifying, ending up in fourth place. But David Coulthard had never been partic-

fifth place, hampered by the loss of the first and second gears, and David Coulthard in sixth. A new front wing configuration was tried out and proved to be successful, with the Finnish driver expressing pleasure in the better handling of the car. This result moved the boss of Mercedes Motorsport, Norbert Haug, to predict that the team could finish the championship in second place.

The British Grand Prix was another good race for McLaren. Mika Hakkinen took third place and a spot on the podium alongside Jacques Villeneuve who gatecrashed Damon Hill's love-in and repayed him for his win at the Canadian race. McLaren opted to

ularly happy with the shorter car. The team went to the trouble of organizing what amounted to a special test session for the Scot in France in order to get him more comfortable with the more 'nervous' disposition of the MP4/11B on the eve of the British race. Though unable to match his team mate's pace, Coulthard managed to slice his way through the field and finish in the points, in fifth place. The race saw the revival of Gerhard Berger, who finally managed to take his Benetton into second place at the finish. But considering the team were running the same engine as Renault, the season so far had been a huge disappointment for the

Anglo-Italian outfit.

The German Grand Prix is home ground for Mercedes and the Stuttgart marque made a special effort to produce an engine better suited for qualifying. Mika Hakkinen qualified in fourth place, another good showing for him, while David Coulthard was back in seventh. In the race the Finn was sidelined by a defective gearbox while the Scot finished once more in the points, behind Damon Hill, Jean Alesi and Jacques Villeneuve.

McLaren was hanging in there, slowly improving, but unable to do anything about the extraordinary combination of Williams, Renault, Hill and Villeneuve. Hungary, where Hakkinen was fourth while Coulthard had to retire on lap 24 due to an engine failure, was where the Williams drivers finished in an elegant, as well as arrogant, one-two to seal the Constructor's Championship for the eighth time, equalling Ferrari's record. This has been an historic period of dominance which Williams and Renault have exerted over Formula One.

As the season reached its climax with the final four races, in Belgium, Italy, Portugal and Japan, it was by no means clear cut who was going to take the driver's championship. The competition still hung in the balance at the very last race in Suzuka, with Williams drivers Damon Hill and Jacques Villeneuve pitted against each other. Ultimately it was Hill in his last race for Williams who kept his nerve and seized the championship. Hill's next season with Arrows will surely be another test of character, and there is little doubt that Villeneuve will start in poll position in the 1997 Championship.

High tech screens help the spectators keep track of positional changes during the race.

Mobil
Leading Technology for Fuel and
Synthetic Lubricants
Technology PARTNER
McLaren
J504 RBM
Mercedes-Benz
Motorsport
Mercedes-Benz
Marlboro
Marlboro
GOODYEAR
EAGLE

Logistics

Three of the five Marlboro, McLaren, Mercedes race trucks.

One of the most arresting sites for someone who comes to a Formula One race is at the back of the pits. The line of gleaming articulated trucks, perfectly parked, facing into the paddock, form an extraordinary backdrop to the circus that is a Formula One Grand Prix weekend. Each team has at least two massive articulated lorries, called race trucks, plus a support vehicle.

McLaren will also have the engine manufacturer's, as well as the fuel supplier's own truck. This means that the team can quite literally take the factory workshop to each Grand Prix of the Formula One World Championships which take place in Europe. For the races outside Europe all of this is transported by air. Each team is completely self-contained, able to operate just as efficiently whether at Silverstone, Monza, Melbourne or São Paulo. McLaren will take three cars and enough spares to fully build another. The race cars are transported in the lorries, which are purpose-built to individual specifications. In addition to this, a top outfit like Marlboro McLaren Mercedes will also take three motor homes, used partly for marketing purposes, and partly as catering centres for the different components of the race team.

About 60 people make up the race team. This may vary, depending on a number of factors, but there will always be a core, comprising the team manager, the team co-ordinator, the chief mechanic and his mechanics, electronic and engine technicians, media, marketing and catering personnel.

It takes numerous trucks to deliver the Formula One circus to each Grand Prix circuit.

The travel arrangements for all of these people, including the journeys to the many test sessions, are the responsibility of a dedicated department at Woking, headed by Jo Ramirez, the team co-ordinator. He and his staff handle thousands of hotel and flight bookings, last minute changes, and many, many dramas, including lost passports, customs disputes, broken-down trucks and double – even treble – hotel and flight overbooking. And then there are helicopters, private jets, courtesy cars, hire cars and so on. It is a non-stop operation which has to be run with military efficiency so that any last minute changes, and there are many, can be accommodated in the schedule.

It's possible that a hotel that has always taken bookings for McLaren's management and the company's VIP guests, can send a fax, a few days before a big race, cancelling all the bookings. This happened in Italy, at the time of the Monza Grand Prix in 1995. Outraged protestations from McLaren were met with an embarrassed admission by the luxury hotel that the Italian government had requisitioned a number of rooms as Yasser Arafat would be staying there. This was one of the very few times that the Mighty McLaren backed out of a fight over hotel bookings.

A number of teams overbook, especially for prestigious races like Monaco, and are desperate to unload these rooms at the last moment. There is a whole sub-culture in the paddock of people trading rooms, passes, hire cars and even team clothing. McLaren generally frowns upon all of this. Regarding team clothing, it is expressly forbidden for McLaren team members to sell it after races, especially the last one or two of the year. This has long been a way for the mechanics to make a little money on the side, and indeed impress some of the local ladies with these fashion accessories. Thus there was much mirth and cackling in the McLaren pits at a

Japanese Grand Prix when an Oriental gentleman, who clearly was not Ron Dennis, the team's most famous member and the issuer of the 'no sale' edict, was seen proudly wearing a beautifully laundered and pressed authentic team shirt with the name 'Ron Dennis' embroidered neatly on it.

For a European race, the two race trucks, plus the fuel truck, will leave Woking on the Monday and arrive at the site of the Grand

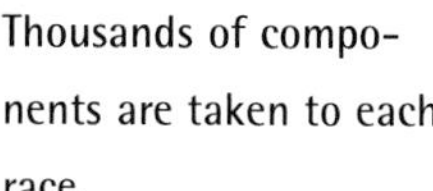

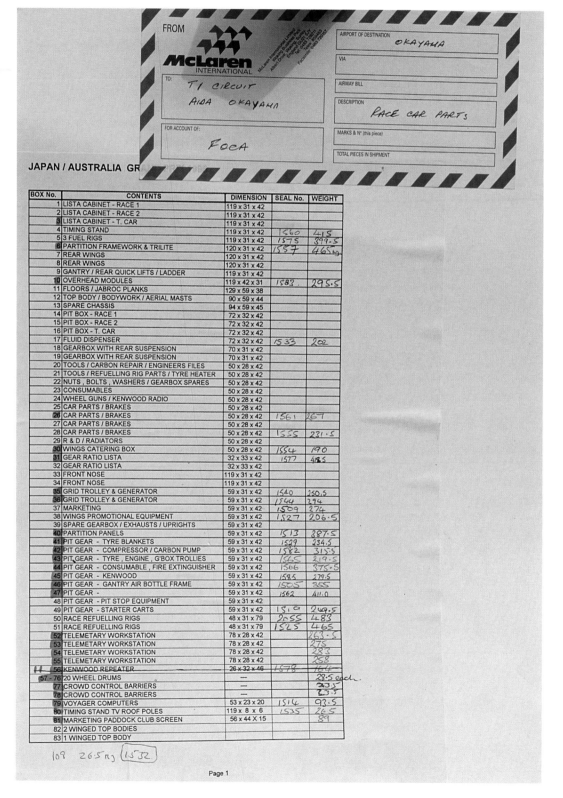

JAPAN / AUSTRALIA GR

BOX No.	CONTENTS	DIMENSION	SEAL No.	WEIGHT
1	LISTA CABINET - RACE 1	119 x 31 x 42		
2	LISTA CABINET - RACE 2	119 x 31 x 42		
3	LISTA CABINET - T. CAR	119 x 31 x 42		
4	TIMING STAND	119 x 31 x 42	1560	415
5	3 FUEL RIGS	119 x 31 x 42	1575	399.5
6	PARTITION FRAMEWORK & TRILITE	120 x 31 x 42	1557	465kg
7	REAR WINGS	120 x 31 x 42		
8	REAR WINGS	120 x 31 x 42		
9	GANTRY / REAR QUICK LIFTS / LADDER	119 x 31 x 42		
10	OVERHEAD MODULES	119 x 42 x 31	1583.	295.5
11	FLOORS / JABROC PLANKS	129 x 59 x 38		
12	TOP BODY / BODYWORK / AERIAL MASTS	90 x 59 x 44		
13	SPARE CHASSIS	94 x 59 x 45		
14	PIT BOX - RACE 1	72 x 32 x 42		
15	PIT BOX - RACE 2	72 x 32 x 42		
16	PIT BOX - T. CAR	72 x 32 x 42		
17	FLUID DISPENSER	72 x 32 x 42	1533	202
18	GEARBOX WITH REAR SUSPENSION	70 x 31 x 42		
19	GEARBOX WITH REAR SUSPENSION	70 x 31 x 42		
20	TOOLS / CARBON REPAIR / ENGINEERS FILES	50 x 28 x 42		
21	TOOLS / REFUELLING RIG PARTS / TYRE HEATER	50 x 28 x 42		
22	NUTS , BOLTS , WASHERS / GEARBOX SPARES	50 x 28 x 42		
23	CONSUMABLES	50 x 28 x 42		
24	WHEEL GUNS / KENWOOD RADIO	50 x 28 x 42		
25	CAR PARTS / BRAKES	50 x 28 x 42		
26	CAR PARTS / BRAKES	50 x 28 x 42	1561	267
27	CAR PARTS / BRAKES	50 x 28 x 42		
28	CAR PARTS / BRAKES	50 x 28 x 42	1555	231.5
29	R & D / RADIATORS	50 x 28 x 42		
30	WINGS CATERING BOX	50 x 28 x 42	1554	190
31	GEAR RATIO LISTA	32 x 33 x 42	1577	48.5
32	GEAR RATIO LISTA	32 x 33 x 42		
33	FRONT NOSE	119 x 31 x 42		
34	FRONT NOSE	119 x 31 x 42		
35	GRID TROLLEY & GENERATOR	59 x 31 x 42	1540	250.5
36	GRID TROLLEY & GENERATOR	59 x 31 x 42	1544	294
37	MARKETING	59 x 31 x 42	1509	274
38	WINGS PROMOTIONAL EQUIPMENT	59 x 31 x 42	1527	206.5
39	SPARE GEARBOX / EXHAUSTS / UPRIGHTS	59 x 31 x 42		
40	PARTITION PANELS	59 x 31 x 42	1513	387.5
41	PIT GEAR - TYRE BLANKETS	59 x 31 x 42	1529	234.5
42	PIT GEAR - COMPRESSOR / CARBON PUMP	59 x 31 x 42	1582	315.5
43	PIT GEAR - TYRE , ENGINE , G'BOX TROLLIES	59 x 31 x 42	1565	219.5
44	PIT GEAR - CONSUMABLE , FIRE EXTINGUISHER	59 x 31 x 42	1566	375.5
45	PIT GEAR - KENWOOD	59 x 31 x 42	1585	279.5
46	PIT GEAR - GANTRY AIR BOTTLE FRAME	59 x 31 x 42	1505	355
47	PIT GEAR -	59 x 31 x 42	1562	411.0
48	PIT GEAR - PIT STOP EQUIPMENT	59 x 31 x 42		
49	PIT GEAR - STARTER CARTS	59 x 31 x 42	1519	249.5
50	RACE REFUELLING RIGS	48 x 31 x 79	2055	483
51	RACE REFUELLING RIGS	48 x 31 x 79	1525	465
52	TELEMETARY WORKSTATION	78 x 28 x 42		263.5
53	TELEMETARY WORKSTATION	78 x 28 x 42		275
54	TELEMETARY WORKSTATION	78 x 28 x 42		283
55	TELEMETARY WORKSTATION	78 x 28 x 42		258
56	~~KENWOOD REPEATER~~	~~26 x 32 x 46~~	~~1578~~	~~164~~
57 - 76	20 WHEEL DRUMS	—		28.5 each.
77	CROWD CONTROL BARRIERS	—		23.5
78	CROWD CONTROL BARRIERS	—		23.5
79	VOYAGER COMPUTERS	53 x 23 x 20	1514	93.5
80	TIMING STAND TV ROOF POLES	119 x 8 x 6	1535	26.5
81	MARKETING PADDOCK CLUB SCREEN	56 x 44 X 15		89
82	2 WINGED TOP BODIES			
83	1 WINGED TOP BODY			

109 26.5kg 1532

Page 1

Thousands of components are taken to each race.

Prix by Tuesday or Wednesday. The pits are then set up and internally built to McLaren's specifications. The floor is painted, high-tech plastic and metal walls and overhead panels – which house electrical and compressed air ducts as well as carrying the team and sponsor logos – are erected, the tool cabinets are fitted, the banks of computer monitors and the processors are also connected. The three motor homes also arrive at about the same

Caps, t-shirts and even ear-plugs have been known to resolve the most complicated linguistic and bureaucratic mis-understandings.

time. Their staff also spend a couple of days converting these vehicles into luxury offices, communication centres and catering units.

On Wednesday an advanced party of the race team arrives by air. This group usually includes the chief mechanic, some mechanics, and one of two electronics engineers, who will be making sure that the computers and the telemetry are in working order by the time the bulk of the team arrives on Thursday.

The marketing and media personnel also arrive on Thursday. McLaren team members all have specifically designed travel clothing supplied by Hugo Boss. At the start of the year this clothing is issued to the 75 or so

Motor homes are used for a variety of purposes, including feeding the team's mechanics for the four days of a meeting.

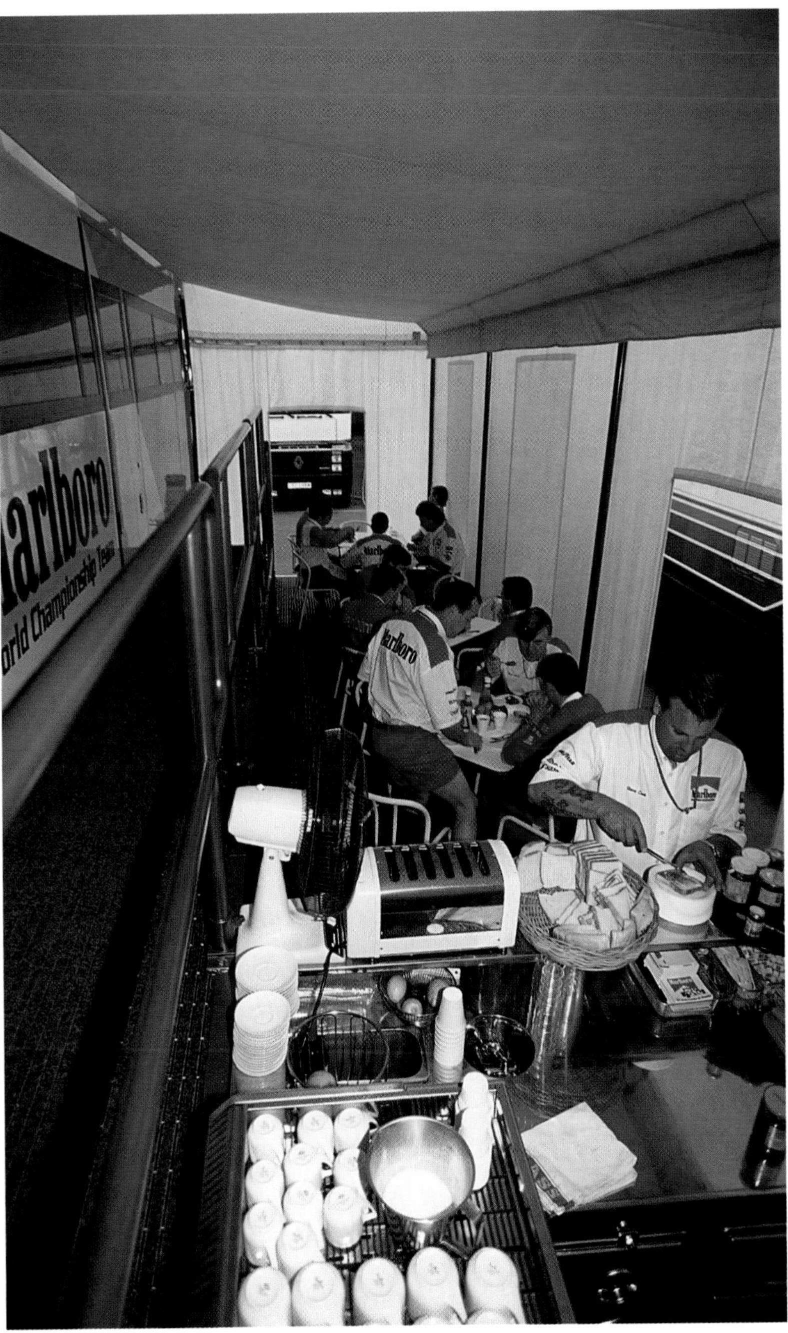

people who are due to travel at some stage in the year. In addition to this, all race team members are issued with the distinctive red-and-white work clothing, which is laundered after every race and test session. In total, 32 items of clothing are issued to each person for every Grand Prix weekend.

Since the introduction of refuelling at the pits, those involved in this must also wear flame-proof overalls, shoes, balaclavas and goggles. All of these items too have to be despatched to every race, making the job of the two employees in the clothing stores as vital and as hectic as any in the Woking factory.

Throughout the race weekend, people will be arriving from Woking carrying the strangest items of hand luggage: if a new nose cone has been designed and manufactured, it is very likely that a late-arriving

Formula One cars are carefully carried in the ingeniously designed race transporters.

Image and neatness of presentation are all vital in Formula One.

team member, usually someone from the marketing company, will be trying to wrestle a bubble-wrapped nose cone down the aisle of a crowded plane. Later there will be much arguing with suspicious customs officials who are desperate to have their moment of glory and impound such a weird-shaped piece of hand baggage. The experienced Formula One team member always has a few souvenirs ready to placate the more awkward customs officials.

This is especially true for the truck drivers who face the nightmarish prospect of being held on the Hungarian border, for example, as officials imply that they will be thoroughly searching their 38-tonne lorries for the next few hours. Caps, t-shirts and even ear plugs have been known to resolve the most complicated linguistic and bureaucratic misunderstandings.

Team manager David Ryan (2nd from right) and systems engineer Dieter Gundel help the race mechanics with the packing up after a race.

Australia

POS	NO.	DRIVER	ENTRANT	RACE TIME	KPH	DIFF
1	5	D.Hill	Rothmans Williams Renault	1:32'50.491	198.736	
2	6	J.Villeneuve	Rothmans Williams Renault	1:33'28.511	197.388	38.020
3	2	E.Irvine	Scuderia Ferrari	1:33'53.062	196.528	1'02.571

FASTEST LAP: 6 J.VILLENEUVE 1:33.421 (204.313 KPH = 126.902 MPH)

Brazil

POS	NO.	DRIVER	ENTRANT	RACE TIME	KPH	DIFF
1	5	D.Hill	Rothmans Williams Renault	1:49'52.976	167.673	
2	3	J.Alesi	Mild Seven Benetton Renault	1:50'10.958	167.217	17.982
3	1	M.Schumacher	Scuderia Ferrari	1:50'00.569	165.122	1 LAP

FASTEST LAP: 5 D.HILL 1'21.547 (190.932 KPH = 118.591 MPH)

Argentina

POS	NO.	DRIVER	ENTRANT	RACE TIME	KPH	DIFF
1	5	D.Hill	Rothmans Williams Renault	1:54'55.322	160.013	
2	6	J.Villeneuve	Rothmans Williams Renault	1:55'07.489	159.731	12.167
3	3	J.Alesi	Mild Seven Benetton Renault	1:55'10.076	159.671	14.754

FASTEST LAP: 3 J.ALESI 1'29.413 (171.478 KPH = 106.508 MPH)

European

POS	NO.	DRIVER	ENTRANT	RACE TIME	KPH	DIFF
1	6	J.Villeneuve	Rothmans Williams Renault	1:33'26.473	196.006	
2	1	M.Schumacher	Scuderia Ferrari	1:33'27.235	195.980	0.762
3	8	D.Coulthard	Marlboro McLaren Mercedes	1:33'59.307	194.865	32.834

FASTEST LAP: 5 D.HILL 1'21.363 (201.585 KPH = 125.208 MPH)

San Marino

POS	NO.	DRIVER	ENTRANT	RACE TIME	KPH	DIFF
1	5	D.Hill	Rothmans Williams Renault	1:35'26.156	193.761	
2	1	M.Schumacher	Scuderia Ferrari	1:35'42.616	193.205	16.460
3	4	G.Berger	Mild Seven Benetton Renault	1:36'13.047	192.187	46.891

FASTEST LAP: 5 D.HILL 1'28.931 (198.032 KPH = 123.001 MPH)

Monaco

POS	NO.	DRIVER	ENTRANT	RACE TIME	KPH	DIFF
1	9	O.Panis	Equipe Ligier Gauloises Blondes	2:00'45.629	124.014	
2	8	D.Coulthard	Marlboro McLaren Mercedes	2:00'50.457	123.931	4.828
3	14	J.Herbert	Red Bull Sauber Ford	2:01'23.132	123.375	37.503

FASTEST LAP: 3 J ALESI 1'25.205 (140.611 KPH = 87.336 MPH)

Spain

POS	NO.	DRIVER	ENTRANT	RACE TIME	KPH	DIFF
1	1	M.Schumacher	Scuderia Ferrari	1:53'47.447	153.785	
2	3	J.Alesi	Mild Seven Benetton Renault	2:00'34.609	152.822	45.302
3	6	J.Villeneuve	Rothmans Williams Renault	2:00'37.695	152.757	48.388

FASTEST LAP: 1 M.SCHUMACHER 1'45.517 (161.274 KPH = 100.170 MPH)

Canada

POS	NO.	DRIVER	ENTRANT	RACE TIME	KPH	DIFF
1	5	D. Hill	Rothmans Williams Renault	1:36'03.465	190.541	
2	6	J. Villeneuve	Rothmans Williams Renault	1:36'07.648	190.402	4.183
3	3	J. Alesi	Mild Seven Benetton Renault	1:36'58.121	188.751	54.656

FASTEST LAP: 6 J. VILLENEUVE 1188.75121.916 (194.291 KPH = 120.678 MPH)

France

POS	NO.	DRIVER	ENTRANT	RACE TIME	KPH	DIFF
1	5	D.Hill	Rothmans Williams Renault	1:36'28.795	190.183	
2	6	J.Villeneuve	Rothmans Williams Renault	1:36'36.922	189.916	8.127
3	3	J.Alesi	Mild Seven Benetton Renault	1:37'15.237	188.669	46.442

FASTEST LAP: 6 J.VILLENEUVE 1'18.610 (194.631 KPH = 120.889 MPH)

Britain

POS	NO.	DRIVER	ENTRANT	RACE TIME	KPH	DIFF
1	6	J.Villeneuve	Rothmans Williams Renault	1:33'00.874	199.576	
2	4	G.Berger	Mild Seven Benetton Renault	1:33'19.900	198.898	19.026
3	7	M.Hakkinen	Marlboro McLaren Mercedes	1:33'51.704	197.775	50.830

FASTEST LAP: 6 J.VILLENEUVE 1'29.288 (204.497 KPH = 127.017 MPH)

Germany

POS	NO.	DRIVER	ENTRANT	RACE TIME	KPH	DIFF
1	5	D.Hill	Rothmans Williams Renault	1:21'43.417	225.410	
2	3	J.Alesi	Mild Seven Benetton Renault	1:21'54.869	224.884	11.452
3	6	J.Villeneuve	Rothmans Williams Renault	1:22'17.343	223.861	33.926

FASTEST LAP: 5 D.HILL 1'46.504 (230.628 KPH = 143.247 MPH)

Hungary

POS	NO.	DRIVER	ENTRANT	RACE TIME	KPH	DIFF
1	6	J.Villeneuve	Rothmans Williams Renault	1:46'21.134	172.372	
2	5	D.Hill	Rothmans Williams Renault	1:46'21.905	172.351	00.771
3	3	J.Alesi	Mild Seven Benetton Renault	1:47'45.346	170.127	1'24.212

FASTEST LAP: 5 D.HILL 1'20.093 (178.352 KPH = 110.777 MPH)

Belgium

POS	NO.	DRIVER	ENTRANT	RACE TIME	KPH	DIFF
1	1	M.Schumacher	Scuderia Ferrari	1:28'15.125	208.442	
2	6	J.Villeneuve	Rothmans Williams Renault	1:28'20.727	208.222	5.602
3	7	M.Hakkinen	Marlboro McLaren Mercedes	1:28'30.835	207.826	15.710

FASTEST LAP: 4 G.BERGER 1'53.067 (221.857 KPH = 137.779 MPH)

Italy

POS	NO.	DRIVER	ENTRANT	RACE TIME	KPH	DIFF
1	1	M.Schumacher	Scuderia Ferrari	1:17'43.632	236.034	
2	3	J.Alesi	Mild Seven Benetton Renault	1:18'01.897	235.113	18.265
3	7	M.Hakkinen	Marlboro McLaren Mercedes	1:18'50.267	232.709	1'06.635

FASTEST LAP: 1 M.SCHUMACHER 1'26.110 (241.226 KPH = 149.830 MPH)

Portugal

POS	NO.	DRIVER	ENTRANT	RACE TIME	KPH	DIFF
1	6	J. Villeneuve	Rothmans Williams Renault	1:40'22.915	182.423	
2	5	D. Hill	Rothmans Williams Renault	1:40'42.881	181.820	19.966
3	1	M. Schumacher	Scuderia Ferrari	1:41'16.680	180.809	53.765

FASTEST LAP: 6 J. VILLENEUVE 1'22.873 (189.398 KPH = 117.638 MPH)

Japan

POS	NO.	DRIVER	ENTRANT	RACE TIME	KPH	DIFF
1	5	D. Hill	Rothmans Williams Renault	1:32'33.791	197.520	
2	1	M. Schumacher	Scuderia Ferrari	1.32'35.674	197.453	1.883
3	7	M. Hakkinen	Marlboro McLaren Mercedes	1:32'37.003	197.405	3.212

FASTEST LAP: 6 J. VILLENEUVE 1'44.043 (202.900 KPH = 126.0248MPH)

ACKNOWLEDGEMENTS

A big thank you to Ken Tyrrell and Harvey Postlethwaite who helped me out of a jam and reminded me once more that Formula One is about fun and not taking oneself too seriously.

Thanks also to Derek Wright and his merry band at Formula One News magazine for their help and lavish hospitality at the Fox & Fornicator.

Crispin Thruston is a fine photographer and a friend. May that be so for a long time.

A very special thanks to the many people at McLaren who helped me: the good bits are theirs, the mistakes are mine. I can't name them due to the draconian laws of silence this Formula One team subscribes to, but the drinks are on me.

Finally, and most importantly, grazie Lalli.

This edition first published in 1996 by Motorbooks
International Publishers & Wholesalers, 729 Prospect Avenue,
PO Box 1, Osceola, WI 54020 USA

Previously published in Great Britain in 1996 by
George Weidenfeld & Nicolson Ltd
London

Library of Congress Cataloguing-in-Publication Data available

ISBN 0-7603-0354-1

Edited by Clare Currie

Designed by Leigh Jones

Litho origination by Pixel Colour, London

Printed and bound by Butler & Tanner,
Frome and London

LOCTITE
8
BOSS
Mobil 1